||||||||||||||||||||||||||||||||||||||||

T0285078

New Teacher Mindset

Practical and Innovative Strategies to Be Different from Day One

Trevor Muir and John Spencer

JB JOSSEY-BASS™
A Wiley Brand

Copyright © 2024 by John Wiley & Sons, Inc. All rights reserved.

Published by John Wiley & Sons, Inc., Hoboken, New Jersey.
Published simultaneously in Canada.

No part of this publication may be reproduced, stored in a retrieval system, or transmitted in any form or by any means, electronic, mechanical, photocopying, recording, scanning, or otherwise, except as permitted under Section 107 or 108 of the 1976 United States Copyright Act, without either the prior written permission of the Publisher, or authorization through payment of the appropriate per-copy fee to the Copyright Clearance Center, Inc., 222 Rosewood Drive, Danvers, MA 01923, (978) 750-8400, fax (978) 750-4470, or on the web at www.copyright.com. Requests to the Publisher for permission should be addressed to the Permissions Department, John Wiley & Sons, Inc., 111 River Street, Hoboken, NJ 07030, (201) 748-6011, fax (201) 748-6008, or online at http://www.wiley.com/go/permission.

Trademarks: Wiley and the Wiley logo are trademarks or registered trademarks of John Wiley & Sons, Inc. and/or its affiliates in the United States and other countries and may not be used without written permission. All other trademarks are the property of their respective owners. John Wiley & Sons, Inc. is not associated with any product or vendor mentioned in this book.

Limit of Liability/Disclaimer of Warranty: While the publisher and author have used their best efforts in preparing this book, they make no representations or warranties with respect to the accuracy or completeness of the contents of this book and specifically disclaim any implied warranties of merchantability or fitness for a particular purpose. No warranty may be created or extended by sales representatives or written sales materials. The advice and strategies contained herein may not be suitable for your situation. You should consult with a professional where appropriate. Further, readers should be aware that websites listed in this work may have changed or disappeared between when this work was written and when it is read. Neither the publisher nor authors shall be liable for any loss of profit or any other commercial damages, including but not limited to special, incidental, consequential, or other damages.

For general information on our other products and services or for technical support, please contact our Customer Care Department within the United States at (800) 762-2974, outside the United States at (317) 572-3993 or fax (317) 572-4002.

Wiley also publishes its books in a variety of electronic formats. Some content that appears in print may not be available in electronic formats. For more information about Wiley products, visit our web site at www.wiley.com.

Library of Congress Cataloging-in-Publication Data

ISBN Names: Muir, Trevor, author. | Spencer, John (Education professor), author.
Title: New teacher mindset: practical and innovative strategies to be
   different from day one / Trevor Muir and John Spencer.
Description: Hoboken, New Jersey: Jossey-Bass, [2024] | Includes index.
Identifiers: LCCN 2024008472 (print) | LCCN 2024008473 (ebook) | ISBN
   9781394210084 (paperback) | ISBN 9781394210107 (adobe pdf) | ISBN
   9781394210091 (epub)
Subjects: LCSH: First year teachers. | Student teachers. | Classroom
   management. | Teacher effectiveness.
Classification: LCC LB2844.1.N4 M84 2024 (print) | LCC LB2844.1.N4
   (ebook) | DDC 370.71/1—dc23/eng/20231207
LC record available at https://lccn.loc.gov/2024008472
LC ebook record available at https://lccn.loc.gov/2024008473

Cover Design: Wiley
Cover Image: © ddok/Shutterstock
Author Photos: (Muir) Photo by Dominic Krupp,
(Spencer) Photo by Betty Boyce Photography

SKY10079752_071824

To Sheri Steelman, who shows me that after 50 years in the classroom you can still be a new teacher.

—Trevor

To my current and past cohort students who continue to bring me hope for the future. You are doing amazing work even when it's hard to see the immediate results.

—John

Contents

Introduction

Let's begin with three stories. See you if you can spot yourself in any of them.

We'll start with Hannah.

Hannah's parents wanted her to become an engineer, but since the age of six when Mrs. Reems told her that she would make a great teacher, that's all she ever wanted to do with her life. Math always seemed to come easy for her, leading to good grades, positive affirmation, and a desire to help others experience the same type of success. If she was honest with herself, she never really understood why some of her friends struggled with calculus. It was like a puzzle to figure out, and she couldn't wait to finish college to help her future students learn to solve the puzzle of calculus as well.

After nailing her job interview, Hannah landed her first teaching job. However, when she was given her first teaching assignment, it wasn't for calculus. Heck, it wasn't even geometry. Hannah was assigned five different classes in the same subject: Algebra 1, and not a single one of them was for honors students.

On day one of her teaching career, she asked her class if anyone could define what rational and irrational numbers are. Hannah was met with blank stares. After a few weeks with her classes, she grew used to those blank stares. Her students were apathetic, often misbehaved, and wanted nothing to do with math class. She offered rewards for effort, threatened consequences,

(continued)

(continued)

devised strategic seating charts to split up the troublemakers, gave out many *D*s and *F*s, and even raised her voice at her class to let them know she meant business, but all her attempts were met with deaf ears.

After a couple of months of this, Hannah sat in her 2004 Honda Civic and cried her eyes out.

"Why didn't I just listen to my parents and get an engineering degree?"

Then, one day, Hannah was venting to an assigned mentor teacher, someone who had been working in schools for over 30 years. The seasoned teacher listened intently to Hannah's honest lament, an outpouring filled with frustration, sadness, and more than anything, self-doubt. With tear-soaked eyes, Hannah cried, "I just don't know why my students hate me."

The veteran teacher saw herself 30 years younger sitting before her, and shared wisdom she wished she would have learned earlier. She said, "Oh, Hannah, your students don't hate you. *They hate math*. You just have to help them understand why they don't have to."

"But how can I do that if I can't even get them to listen to a word I say?" Hannah replied.

"You might just have to teach them a bit *differently* than the way you were taught."

Next is Miguel's story.

Miguel was a *C* student back in the day, and that was mostly because his parents would ground him if he received anything less. He was always placed in "regular" classes, received detentions for distracting other students, and had to take remedial math to get into college. Miguel didn't like school. It wasn't that school was too hard for him; it was just too boring.

The school day usually started off fine, but by 10 a.m., he'd start to fidget at his desk as the teacher lectured in the front of the room. He'd watch the clock on the wall slowly tick down the minutes until lunch, where he'd be allowed to talk to his friends, but only for 20 minutes before he'd be back in a desk, either watching the clock again, or most likely in the afternoon, wandering the hallways of the school on bathroom breaks or throwing pencils across the classroom when the teachers weren't looking.

For Miguel, school meant boredom, and that often led to bad grades, detentions, and a sharp distaste for school.

But Miguel did love to write. Something about it was freeing to him, and language arts was the only area of school he thrived. Because he was expected by his parents to go to college, he chose to be an English major, knowing that would be his only way to get through another four years of classroom boredom.

So of course, he laughed in his professor's face when she suggested he could be a great English teacher someday.

"Why would I do that? I hate school!" Miguel replied.

The professor responded, "But, Miguel, I love the way you write. What if you could teach students how to do that as well, except do it in a way that works for them, maybe a little *differently*?"

This set Miguel on a path he never could have imagined for himself. He became a teacher, but he vowed to never let his students feel the same boredom he experienced for so many years. Instead of drab, blank walls, Miguel covered every square inch with posters that had nothing to do with education. Students regularly asked him who the Dave Matthews Band was, and Miguel always responded by blasting it from the classroom speakers. His students cringed, and Miguel did not care. Miguel gave every student a nickname and had special handshakes with all of them. He jumped on tables when he got excited, banned the use of textbooks in his room, made every unit a massive project, every lesson a hands-on experience, and went to work every day with the singular goal of every student loving school.

And after a few years of teaching like this, *Miguel burned out*.

Sustaining that kind of energy for 180 days straight was beyond Miguel's capacity. And in his attempt to make every learning activity fun, students were always expecting stimulation. And on those inevitable days when class was

(continued)

(*continued*)

not fun, students were apathetic and disengaged. Miguel found himself losing his temper too often as his class devolved into chaos. He saw a sharp rise in behavior issues, and surprisingly, an even higher rise in students who did not want to attend his class. It turns out, the introverts in his room couldn't handle the noise and distraction that comes with a class that is always fun.

Naturally, Miguel began to wonder if there was *any* way to lead a class successfully. He was living proof that the traditional sit-and-get model does not work for many students. Yet, a class based solely on excitement and enjoyment was not working as well. He was either going to have to discover a *different* way of teaching or do something else with his English degree.

The final story is Katie's.

Katie slowly turns the key, pulls down on the doorknob, and inhales the stale classroom air. There's a vague scent of laminated posters and carpet shampoo. But to Katie, it smells like potential. She stares at an empty wall. It's a blank canvas that will soon have student artwork and anchor charts and collective brainstorms of the epic projects her students will do.

She glances at the barricade of furniture pushed to the far side of the room, and pulling out her trusted gel pen and notebook, she sketches an initial plan for how the space will look. How will she make it adaptable and flexible but also consistent? How will she design spaces that maximize collaboration but honor the need for quiet introspection?

A half hour later, she pulls out the Bluetooth speaker and turns to her mixtape. Well, that's what she calls it. In year one, it was an actual cassette. Now, 27 years later, it's a playlist on a streaming app. It's *in the cloud*, a term she couldn't have imagined using nearly three decades ago when she was in teachers college.

When she started, the school had one computer lab with wired internet. She still used an overhead transparency projector and a mimeograph machine, and the students would go nuts when she wheeled in the TV cart.

This year feels different: a new city and a new grade level. But also, she can feel something bigger: a new generation with new needs and new challenges. An artificial intelligence (AI) revolution changing the way people learn and think and create. Then again, Katie often feels like a new teacher. And that's okay. Because each year, she is a new teacher. She's trying new strategies. She's dreaming up new projects. True, she's a veteran. She's an expert. But she never wants to stop innovating.

Katie has lived through a recession, a pandemic, and a set of policies that pushed standardized testing as the ultimate solution. She is resilient, adaptable, and creative.

"I've got this," she mutters to herself, as she sifts through a box of materials. She has piles of notebooks of new ideas that she wants to try out. She has a new escape-room activity her third graders will love. She has a highlighted journal article about emerging research on how to teach phonics. She still can't wait to meet her new students. That list of names will soon be replaced with 27 unique people whose stories she will get to know over the course of the year.

But despite her experience and the successes she has had, Katie feels nervous and even a little scared. It's the same pit she had in her stomach 27 years ago, and every year since.

What if these ideas don't work?
Do I have the energy and stamina for this anymore?
What if I can't figure out the new technology?
Am I too old to be relevant to my students?
What if they don't like me?

But she doesn't let those thoughts linger for long. She's been through this before. She will challenge perceptions and prove that a veteran teacher can be innovative. She will be *different* and her students will remember her forever.

Hi, I'm Trevor.
And I'm John.

We were both raised in an education system that impacted us in many ways. It's where we learned how to read, write, calculate, problem-solve, wonder, socialize, get in trouble, get out of trouble, factor polynomials, deal with bullies, sit for very long periods of time, do all the work on group projects, let someone else do all the work on group projects, write essays, create art, fall in love with reading, and lots of other things that probably impacted you as well.

When you spend 13 years doing anything, it tends to have a formative effect. From kindergarten to senior year, we sat in classrooms and had learning experiences that were a key part in forming our identities, our knowledge, our skills, our development—school helped form us. And it probably did the same for you as well.

So let's start there. School is formative. Whether you were a part of the 1 million students who are homeschooled, the 9 million who go to private school, or the 43 million from public schools, the educational experience is deeply influential.

And perhaps the most formative aspect of education is the people who lead it, those who design and guide their students through learning experiences with the intent of it benefiting them now and thereafter.

For each of us, this was the catalyst for becoming teachers. We both had educators who inspired a deep love of their subject areas, but an even deeper love of learning. These teachers stood out enough in our memories to leave an imprint—something in the way they connected with us, but also helped us connect with what they taught, that inspired us to want to do the same: to start careers as teachers ourselves.

How can we be teachers like them?

However, not all of school was like sitting in Mr. Keating's class in the *Dead Poet's Society*, full of excitement about poetry and confidence to take on the world. Actually, much of school wasn't like that at all. Instead, school was often stale and uninspiring.

We'd sit in rows for seven hours, listen to an adult talk *at* us from the front of the room, and try to remember everything they said long enough to regurgitate it on a test, then repeat.

And starting in about second grade, you even had to go home and do more of that work after those seven hours in school. And if you didn't do it at home, you'd get in trouble when you went back to school, making those 7 hours even more unbearable. Too often, school was about penalties and rewards. It was about learning information without the slightest clue about how it would ever be used in the "real world." Of course, there were teachers like Mr. Feeney, who cared about his students as people first, and everything else followed. Or Mrs. Frizzle, who could light a fire in you about their subject area.

But there were also teachers who had been beaten down from years in a profession that demanded too much and paid too little that they lost the joy in their work. And no student wants to be in a classroom led by someone who has lost their passion for teaching.

School was good.

And school was not.

So we each began our paths to becoming educators, at different times and places, but both with the objective to be impactful teachers for our future students, knowing the education system isn't perfectly designed to support this objective. But to do this, we knew we'd have to think *differently* about teaching.

We were filled with hope and optimism that we could do it, that we can lead students toward a deep love for learning, wondering, and creating that they would hold on to long after their time in our classrooms. Dare I say, we were idealistic, ready to become the teachers our students need. So after college, teacher training, student teaching, and countless sleepless nights, we became teachers.

And we quickly learned that there is a stark difference between ideals and reality. We'll dive into this reality throughout the book, but let's sum it up here:

Teaching is challenging.

It's complex, messy, and part of a massive system that is often slow to change. As new teachers, it took us both time to learn how to thrive in this system and work with all of the complexity and messiness. To be the kind of teachers we wanted to be, to teach in a culture and climate that is constantly changing, to adapt to new technologies, to push against the education system while also existing and thriving within it, we would have to think *different* and be *different*.

We, along with most who have stepped foot in a classroom, can identify with the three stories at the beginning of this Introduction. We've been in Hannah's shoes, and tried everything under the sun to engage our students, only to come up empty. Like Miguel, we've wanted classrooms to be a boredom-free zone, but also have seen what happens when you try to make school fun and exciting every moment of the day. We understand the excitement of Katie as she approaches day one of the school year, and the nerves that go along with trying new approaches to teaching. We've realized that sometimes what we've learned just doesn't always work, and we have to discover a different approach.

Now, *different* doesn't always mean bold or flashy. It doesn't mean ditching everything that's been done in education and replacing it with something brand-new. There's power in so many "traditional" teaching practices and wisdom to be gained from seasoned educators. But *different* also doesn't mean resisting change and refusing to adapt while everyone else moves forward.

Different is about embracing what works, but paying attention to new research, being open to new ideas, and being adaptable in an ever-changing world. It means not ignoring the fact that there was a global pandemic, increasing societal and political pressure, or the introduction of AI technology at our fingertips. It's recognizing that the world is changing and adjusting accordingly.

It's a mindset.

When you are different from day one, you are willing to take creative risks. You know that every lesson is an experiment. It might not work perfectly at first, but through many tiny iterations, your lessons grow more effective and innovative. As a result, you grow more adaptable in the face of change.

And change is inevitable, especially in the world of education. Because of this, we have to pivot, adapt, innovate, sometimes swim against the current, discover new practices, identify ones that need to be retained despite shifting currents—we need to be a different kind of teacher.

So if you're brand-new to this profession, welcome. We're excited to be on this journey with you. And if you've been here a while, remember that you're always a new teacher, whether it's year 1 or 31. Every year will be a new year with a new group of students and a chance to try new strategies and design new systems. Every day will be a new chance to innovate and iterate and make something different. Every day is another day one and a chance to be *different*.

Building Relationships from Day One

CHAPTER

1

Building Relationships
from Day One

It was the first Friday of the first week of my first year as a teacher and I (John) was determined to have students engage in a hands-on learning activity. My students were going to solidify their understanding of the five themes of geography by creating collages that represent each of them. I had spent weeks asking friends and family for old magazines. I hit up every back-to-school sale, and purchased an absurd amount of glue and cardstock and tempera paints.

I showed up two hours early to set out the supplies. I photocopied the detailed instructions that I had reworked over and over again. I stopped for a moment to daydream about what this would look like someday when they made a teacher movie about my story. The students would fall in love with social studies through hands-on learning. They would discover the joy of geography and learn that history wasn't something in the past; it was alive in the present.

This was going to be epic.

The first week was a success up to this point. I knew almost every student's name. I talked about sports and video games and music with the students who gathered by my door before class. We were becoming a community, and today I would take it to the next level with a hands-on learning experience. My stomach turned with that mix of excitement and anxiety as I stared at the clock waiting for the morning bell to ring.

As the students streamed in, I could sense their confusion. No warm-up? No bell work? What's with all the paints and magazines?

"Today is going to be different," I told them. I launched into an excited pitch for our mini-project and ended with a quick reminder about classroom rules and consequences. Then, I let them loose.

My first two classes finished early, which meant most students wandered around talking while I frantically looked for places for the paint to dry. In between class periods, I fought back a lingering sense of disappointment. This wasn't epic. It was a collage. It wasn't the stuff of the silver screen super-teachers. It was a craft. But still, students were generally engaged and that was a success for a Friday. I tempered my expectations a bit, but still hoped that one of my classes would live up to my hopes for this project.

In my third class period, a group of students decided to smear paint on their faces. Right after sending them to the restroom, I heard a loud crash and the shattering of glass. I spun around to see a girl crying as she pulled broken shards from her hair.

"Who did this?" I growled.

The class remained silent.

"Just own up to it! Who did this?" I screamed. I know in teacher circles we often say, "I lost my voice" as code for yelling, but this was screaming. I was red in the face. And once I calmed down, I made every student write down who did it. One name emerged over and over again—Jose.

I wasn't surprised. Teachers had warned me about Jose before school began. So, I wrote the referral and sent him to the office. During lunch, I stopped by the office and Jose insisted that he hadn't done anything wrong.

"I don't want to hear it. There are witnesses," I responded.

But as I headed back to my class, a quiet girl pulled me aside and said, "Mr. Spencer, I need to tell you something." Tears were streaming down her face.

"Maria, what's wrong? Did something happen to you?"

"It was me. I knocked down the picture. I was trying to toss glue to a friend and it accidentally hit the picture. It wasn't Jose."

She walked with me to the office and I apologized to Jose and his mother, embarrassed by how I handled this situation. This moment shaped the way I thought about discipline forever.

Five Truths about Building Effective Relationships

I share this story as a disclaimer that I don't have this all figured out. Trevor and I both have cringe-worthy moments when we raised our voices at our classes (code word for yelled) or accidentally shamed them or simply didn't know how to get a loud and rowdy group to settle down.

In teachers college, we both read books that promised we would have "no classroom management issues" if we followed the directions laid out in the pages. We wrote essays in college describing how we'd incorporate these directions in our classroom management plan, modeled these methods in front of our professors and other preservice teachers, and memorized the directions as if they were answers on a test.

And then we started teaching and followed the directions to a tee, and quite often, they simply didn't work. At first, we thought it was us. Maybe we weren't consistent enough. Perhaps we hadn't mastered the right techniques. We wondered if we simply weren't talented enough as teachers.

Eventually, we realized, through our own unique journeys, that there is no instruction manual for classroom management. We are all messy humans in a messy world. Our classrooms will always have tension and conflict and challenges. It's the nature of working with people. That's what makes it hard, but it's also what makes it beautiful.

We came into teaching with a traditional mindset toward classroom management. We had a system of punishments and rewards, and expected every student to follow the rules we set up. We thought if we had clear rules and logical consequences for misbehavior, our classrooms would run smoothly.

And I'm not going to lie, sometimes it worked. Sometimes class was smooth and students did follow our instructions. But then inevitable conflict would arise. A student would have an outburst. There was a fight in the hallway right before class. Some students didn't follow our rules. There was a full moon. (If that doesn't make sense now, teach for a while and you'll get it.)

Or we'd lose our temper on a kid who turned out to be innocent.

And it became apparent that simply having rules, rewards, and penalties was not sufficient. All of the rules and procedures in the world could not negate the fact that teaching is inherently messy. This realization began our journeys to discover a better way to manage our classrooms.

We now view classroom management through a different, and perhaps, more realistic lens: that teaching is relational. Like all relationships, there's no instruction manual or map to guide you down the perfect path.

Relationships are messy.

So, instead of offering an instruction manual, we'd like to share some counterintuitive truths about classroom management that we have seen in our own classrooms.

Truth #1: There's Strength in Humility

Jose didn't even look up when I apologized to him. The principal attempted to get him to acknowledge me, but he turned away and stared at the wall. He had every right to be angry. I hadn't simply made a mistake. I made a snap judgment based on a child's reputation. In my own fear and insecurity, I lashed out at that class and failed to listen to Jose's side of the story.

The next day, I apologized again. Jose's response was, "That's okay. I'm used to this."

"It's not okay and I don't want you to get used to this. I am genuinely sorry," I answered.

For the next week, Jose looked away and avoided eye contact. But subtly something changed. He answered a question. He joined his group discussion. He turned in an assignment. Then, to my surprise, when I invited him to join the cross-country team, he asked if he could call his mom and see if his aunt could babysit his younger sister so he could come to try-outs.

Over the course of the year, Jose emerged as a leader in my class. There were still moments when I gently redirected him and a few times when he got into fights at lunch time or in physical education (PE) class. However, he also thrived in small group settings where he was natural project manager. One day, a teacher across the breezeway dropped a beaker and the glass shattered. He looked up at me and said, "Hey, Mr. Spencer, I swear that wasn't me. No matter how many people write my name on a paper."

While I still cringe at the way I judged Jose, he was able to turn the incident into an inside joke because he had truly forgiven me. This was a reminder that there's strength in humility. I remember being worried that apologizing might be seen as a sign of weakness to students. Would they simply walk all over me afterward? But in my experience, students typically respond with kindness. They view an apology as a sign of strength. This humility is ultimately what allows teachers and students to restore their relationships.

There's strength in humility.

Truth #2: Classroom Management Is Deeply Relational

Often new teachers are told, "Don't take student behavior personally." It's not you; it's them. If a student is talking while you're talking, they might simply want to chat with a neighbor. When a student comes in grumpy and snaps at you, it's often connected to something on the playground or the lunch room.

While it's true that we shouldn't *take* behavior personally, classroom management *is* personal because it connects to relationships. The incident with Jose wasn't merely a discipline issue. It was a relational one. One student felt that she couldn't get up and move in my classroom and she was afraid to ask. She threw paint across the room out of a fear of breaking the rules. A group of students blamed one particular student for breaking a picture frame because he had always been labeled as the troublemaker. I lashed out at the entire class and blamed one specific student. These moments were all deeply relational. I had hurt my students by getting angry, shaming a student, and failing to listen. I wasn't even sure how I would fix things.

Moving forward, my goal was to restore the relationship with my students and to improve their relationships with one another. One of the most effective methods of cultivating positive classroom relationships is using the Establish-Maintain-Restore (EMR) process (see Figure 1.1).

FIGURE 1.1 The EMR method.

Source: Cook, C. R., Coco, S., Zhang, Y., Fiat, A. E., Duong, M. T., Renshaw, T. L., Long, A. C., & Frank, S. (2018). Cultivating positive teacher–student relationships: Preliminary evaluation of the establish–maintain–restore (EMR) method. APA PsycNet. https://psycnet.apa.org/record/2018-47899-002" with "Adapted from Cook et.al. 2018. https://psycnet.apa.org/record/2018-47899-002.

This starts with teachers establishing positive relationships with students, maintaining them throughout the year, and after inevitable conflict (because teaching is messy), restoring the relationship with students.

In *Cultivating Positive Teacher-Student Relationships*, researchers conducted a blind study with fourth- and fifth-grade teachers to analyze the connection between student-teacher relationships and positive behavior.[1] They found that teachers who used the Establish-Maintain-Restore process in their classrooms saw "significant improvement in student outcomes" and a sharp drop in disruptive behavior. Another group studied the effect Establish-Maintain-Restore has on student outcomes, including "improvements in academic achievement and engagement and reductions in disruptive behaviors, suspension, and risk of dropping out."[2] Universally, programs that use EMR saw the largest effects on overall student outcomes.

This makes sense. Students who feel invested in, trusted, and respected by their teachers have a different posture toward being in class. The point of student-teacher relationships is not to *just* be kind and friendly to students, it's the bedrock for classroom management. When their attitudes are oriented in this way, more time and energy is devoted to academics and less to managing and correcting negative behavior.

Truth #3: There Are No Good or Bad Students

I (Trevor) once had a student in my class named Dave who I initially perceived as being lazy, and maybe even a little rude. He never raised his hand to speak in class, avoided eye contact when I spoke to him, turned in less than half of his assignments, and I constantly caught him watching YouTube videos on his laptop when he was supposed to be working. I exercised so much patience with Dave, and yet he would still just shrug his shoulders when I asked him why he wasn't working. It was only a couple of weeks into the school year when I filed a place for Dave in my mind on the "bad kid" list. Of course, I didn't think he was purely bad, but if I'm being honest, he was easy to classify as difficult and possibly unreachable.

After a couple of months of this, I'd had enough and decided to call home to let his parents know. A woman answered who I thought to be Dave's mother, and I said to her, "I'm Dave's teacher, and I'm really struggling to get Dave to participate in class and was hoping you could give me some suggestions."

She replied, "Hi Mr. Muir, I'm not Dave's mother, I'm his foster mom. And we've been having the same issues since he's been with us. I've actually been meaning to call you hoping you could give me some advice."

Oh, I didn't know Dave was in foster care.

Dave's foster mom proceeded to share with me that Dave holds the record at his social work agency for being in the most homes in the shortest amount of time. She told me a little bit about why he was in foster care and some of the horrible things that were done to him and how this has all had a deep impact on the way he interacts with adults, especially men.

This was heartbreaking. I had no idea that Dave wasn't lazy; he was angry, sad, and hurt. I ended that call without any specific answers as to how to get Dave to engage in my class. However, I gained a deep empathy for the student whom I had improperly labeled.

And when I remember this, I can see that a "bad kid" is often someone in pain. At the same time, I am not surprised when a "good kid" does something bad. Behavior is communication. Sometimes a lazy student is really an insecure student. Sometimes a tired student is really a hungry one. Sometimes a rude, misbehaving student is really an insecure one, and would rather get in trouble than fail at their task. Sometimes a student who says hurtful things to their teacher is actually hurting themselves, and the words they sling are really a reaction to their own pain.

Behavior is communication.

A student's life experience does not excuse poor behavior or make it any less distracting/hurtful, but it does explain it. And one of the most challenging, yet important roles of an educator, is to recognize the fact that students are communicating through their actions and to react accordingly. The reality is, every single behavior in school has an explanation.

This might seem theoretical, but this mindset can help us think differently about discipline. First, it means you are open to the idea that you might not know the whole story. It never hurts to delay judgment and gather facts slowly before choosing a course of action with discipline. In addition, it means you are willing to work with challenging students because you know they are capable of growth. Finally, it's a daily reminder that you will hold all students to a high standard of behavior while also recognizing that students are going to mess up along the way.

Truth #4: Classroom Management Is a Learning Opportunity

The traditional, behaviorist view of classroom management holds that students behave based on a system of punishments and rewards. If teachers use the right reinforcements with students, they can maximize ideal behavior while limiting challenging behaviors. We see this approach with schoolwide discipline initiatives like Positive Behavior Interventions and Supports (PBIS), and through token rewards systems.

But ultimately, what is the goal of classroom management? You might want to see students learn self-regulation and impulse control. Perhaps you want students to learn how to navigate conflict and solve interpersonal issues. Maybe you're hoping for personal integrity and honesty. Chances are, it's a combination of factors that can be summed up with the idea of "doing the right thing because it's the right thing to do." In other words, we want students to do the right thing, not for a prize, but because of an intrinsic motivation.

This is why it helps to treat discipline issues as learning opportunities. We'll take a deeper dive into this topic in the next chapter, but the big idea is that we can treat discipline issues as opportunities for students to self-reflect, set goals, and grow. Like PBIS and other rewards systems, this growth equates to better behavior, but now the motivation is students developing elemental transformation rather than following a carrot on a stick. We might still need to provide consequences and incentives, but we can approach these interactions with the question, "What do I want this student to learn from this experience?"

Practical Ideas: Getting to Know Students

As a new teacher, I (Trevor) had my students write "I'm From" poems, an activity where students share their life stories in poetry. For some students, this was a fun way to share about their home-lives and contexts. However, many kids would skip this assignment, and it was often because this activity wasn't trauma-informed. Not every student feels safe sharing their story. While vulnerability has a place in the classroom, it can take months to develop trust as a community, and students should have a sense of control over how much they are sharing. I needed to shift get-to-know-you activities from personal experiences to geeky interests. Starting with student interests can help build student confidence by sending the message that we are all experts in something. This creates a culture where students are able to learn from one another from day one.

When getting to know your students, perhaps start with impersonal activities, like scavenger hunts, escape rooms, or trivia games. Then begin to move to more personal activities, like interest surveys, show-and-tell, or autobiographical writing assignments.

We tend to do "get-to-know-you" activities at the start of the school year but then move into core content afterward. However, if we integrate more personal get-to-know-you activities throughout the school year, students can more naturally learn about one another as they build trust over time.

Ten Ways to Get to Know Your Students

The personal connection is critical for both customized learning and classroom leadership. Here are 10 was to get to know your students better as people:

1. **Sporting events:** Visit sporting events. This will allow you to see both the athletes and the spectators in a different light. It's also a chance to mingle with families.

2. **Home visits:** I find that when I do home visits, I am reminded that students come from real homes with real families. I see students through a more holistic lens.

3. **Clubs:** Many clubs hold competitions. Sometimes they are sparsely attended. I know, people are crazy enough to think that kids tackling one another is more exciting than a debate competition. Showing up to these can be a real morale booster for students.

4. **Sponsor:** Go beyond simply visiting club competitions and sporting events and volunteer to be the coach or sponsor of one. This allows you to play the role of leader in a realm that is outside the traditional classroom setting.

5. **Pop culture:** Spend a little time (emphasis on *little*) listening to the music, watching the movies, or checking out the TV shows that your students do. It's not critical that you are up-to-date, but it does give you a picture of how marketers view the youth that you work with.

6. **Personal element to assignments:** Give students a chance to tell their stories, share their beliefs, and use their talents in assignments.

7. **Small talk:** Use the time spent on duty, standing outside your door or walking students to and from lunch as a chance to engage in small talk. Often, the talk is nowhere near as small as you might think.

8. **Transparency:** When you are humble and willing to admit mistakes, you allow students to let down their guard and share what's really going on in life.

9. **Conferences:** Some students will easily slip through the cracks if a teacher doesn't schedule one-on-one conferences. Sometimes all it takes is three five-minute conferences a day and you've met with every student in a two-week period.

10. **Surveys:** Start the school year off with surveys or learning inventories that allow you to see a student's personality, beliefs, interests, and talents.

Note that you don't need to do all of these things. Chaperoning a dance might not be your thing, and that's okay. The point is that when we gear intentionality toward building and fostering relationships with our students, we are making an investment in their learning. And not just learning in terms of how to act socially and in relationships.

Building student-teacher relationships with students isn't just to be kind. We have to shift the mindset on this. Relationships are not an optional addition to the delivery of content and the teaching of skills.

Instead, they are the foundation for all of the learning and interactions that happen in your classroom throughout the school year. The connection you form with students forms a pathway between you and them, but also the content of your class and their minds. A relationally engaged student is often an academically engaged one. Of course it's imperfect. You'll say the wrong thing. Students can hurt your feelings. You can hurt theirs. There will be conflict. It will be messy.

But name anything memorable that didn't get a little messy first. Access the Get to Know You Survey at newteachermindset.com.

Notes

1. Cook, C. R., Coco, S., Zhang, Y., Fiat, A. E., Duong, M. T., Renshaw, T. L., Long, A. C., and Frank, S. (2018). Cultivating positive teacher-student relationships: Preliminary evaluation of the establish–maintain–restore (EMR) method. *APA PsycNet*. https://psycnet.apa.org/record/2018-47899-002
2. Kincade, Laurie, Cook, Clayton, and Goerdt, Annie. (2020). Meta-analysis and common practice elements of universal approaches to improving student-teacher relationships. *Sage Journals*. https://journals.sagepub.com/doi/abs/10.3102/0034654320946836

Proactive Classroom Management: A Preventative Approach to Behavioral Issues

When I (Trevor) was a brand-new teacher, I looked very young for my age. At my first parent-teacher conference, a parent came to my classroom and asked where the teacher was. I looked like the Karate Kid, but not the adult Ralph Macchio version, instead a skinny 24-year-old who people would often mistake for a sophomore.

A professor told me during my teacher prep program that looking so young can make it difficult for students to take you seriously. So he offered me some sage wisdom given to many teachers before me: "Don't smile until Christmas."

Essentially, he said you cannot warm up to the students too quickly and let your guard down or else they will walk all over you. Smiling, goofing off, having fun, or cracking a joke will send a message to students that the teacher isn't serious about learning.

Students will act crazy. Chaos will ensue. Desks will fly. Trash cans will burn. You get the idea.

This professor told me that the first half of the school year needs to be strict and rigid; the teacher needs to refrain from jokes and laughing until students know, without a doubt, that you command respect.

This advice made sense to me, as I terrorized a number of young-looking teachers in my high school days. However, teaching in this way was totally counter to my nature. My initial spark to become a teacher was to make school a place students wanted to be. Learning this famous idiom felt conflicting as I really didn't want to be walked on by my students, so I decided early on to take that professor's advice.

Don't Smile Until Christmas

In that first fall in the classroom, I had a student named Sara in my English class who refused to listen to me. I kindly asked her twice to wake up and stop sleeping during my lesson. The work we were covering was complex and important for her to learn, and there was no way for her to learn it if she was sleeping in the back of the classroom. Both times I tapped her desk and kindly asked her to wake up; she'd pop up her head and apologize, but soon after fall back asleep.

The third time I caught her sleeping in that class period, I decided that it was time to lose my cool a little and make sure she understands how serious I am about staying awake in my class. I felt like her repeated sleeping was misbehavior, and that warning from my college professor was coming to fruition.

And so I yelled at Sara.

From across the room.

In front of everyone.

Loud.

I yelled, "This isn't nap time; it's English class, I need you to wake up!"

And I have to say, that girl popped her head up quickly and kept it up the rest of class. She even pulled out her book and worked a little that day, so I couldn't help but think that even though I'm a new teacher, I've got classroom management down! I have to stop being Mr. Nice Guy and make an example out of students to make a point. And it was clear that point was made as all of the students in the room froze when I reprimanded Sara and then looked to me with wide eyes. They were clearly thinking, "That 12-year-old teacher means business!"

Maybe the professor in teaching college was right that *I should not smile until Christmas.*

At the end of class, I approached Sara, and asked her why she keeps falling asleep in my class.

She again said, "Sorry, Mr. Muir," and I replied, "No, you keep telling me you're sorry, but then you keep doing it. I need to know why you're not working."

She looked at me with tired, wet eyes and quietly told me that her little sister had an asthma attack the evening before, and that her inhaler had run out. And since her dad works third shift and her mom hasn't been around in over a year, she had to call 911 and ride in the ambulance to the hospital with her little sister. Sara told me that her dad picked her up that morning from the hospital and dropped her off at school.

Her response took the wind out of me.

You can imagine how I felt at that moment. This girl who experienced hell the night before, who practically raises her little sister and desperately needed rest, was shamed by her teacher in front of everyone. It was a punch to the gut, and all I could say in that moment was that I was sorry. Sorry for what she had to go through and for how I treated her.

There's Always More Beneath the Surface

As much as I hate thinking about this story, I also know that this moment early in my career served as a catalyst. It was where I developed a new mindset around getting to know students, becoming aware of the fact that students are not just blank slates when they walk into our rooms, but instead are living out stories. And these stories have very real conflict. Whether the conflict has trauma like I learned Sara's did or if it's the pressures/distractions/temptations that come with being a kid in the 21st century, there is always more than meets the eye with students. This is why when we think about classroom management, this fact has to be considered above all else.

The reality that students are every bit as human as the rest of us cannot be understated. It is the baseline for all connections and interactions in the classroom. It's like icebergs and how only a small portion is revealed above the surface. The same is true for students. There is always, without exception, an explanation for student behavior. As said in the previous chapter, this doesn't always excuse negative behavior, but it does shed light on to why it happens.

Proactive Classroom Management Begins with Recognizing Your Students' Stories

Classroom management is often seen as strategies and theories to best maintain a group of students. While partially true, this "traditional" mindset fails to consider the benefits of taking a proactive approach to classroom management. Before any strategy should be employed, we have to realize this reality of our students. Your empathy for your students will impact your management, pedagogy, and even curriculum. We will get into all of that later in the book. But for now, let it be the baseline, the starting point for all classroom management.

A Proactive Approach to Classroom Management

Again, humans are messy. Students walk in with trauma and baggage, and even in the perfect environment (and news flash: there is no perfect environment), you'll still run into issues. Even the most amazing master teachers you meet will experience classroom management snags.

However, while we cannot prevent all behavioral issues from occurring, we can be proactive in our approach. The following are typical problems you might run into and how you can take a more proactive approach.

Problem #1: Students Are Bored

Sometimes students get off-task because they are bored. In some cases, they find the subject irrelevant.

In elementary school, I (Trevor . . . but probably everyone reading this) used to count the holes in the drop ceiling panels of my classroom. Usually in math class, I'd get lost in a daze meticulously counting every single one, and when I'd finish one panel, I'd just move to the next. In middle school, I'd do the same thing, but eventually learned how to fling a pencil into one of those holes. My teachers would usually come tap on my desk to snap me out of my comatose state, but what usually snapped me out of it was either the poor grades on quizzes following those lessons, or the detentions I'd get for flinging pencils into the ceiling.

This behavior was not an act of rebellion nor was it even obstinance, although I have plenty of those examples as well. Instead, it was driven by boredom. Often in classes where the purpose of the learning and work was not articulated to me, and therefore, I had no interest in it, I would search for stimulation elsewhere.

This isn't to say students need to be entertained at all times or that a teacher's job is to eradicate all traces of boredom. It is not realistic nor is it actually beneficial to eliminate all boredom from school (more on that in Chapter 8). But there is often a strong correlation between boredom and student behavior. In research published by the *Educational Psychology Review*, researchers discovered "a significant differential impact of boredom on academic motivation, study strategies and behaviors, and achievement."[1] Therefore, we have to consider the role boredom can play in misbehavior.

Sometimes boredom comes from a lack of challenge. Students have already mastered the standards and feel frustrated by the repetition of the content, so they disrupt the learning process.

The Solution: Focus on Intrinsic Motivation

When students are bored, we need to consider how we can craft lessons to be more engaging. Researcher Philip Schlechty describes this shift from "strategic compliance," where students play the game of school, to "true engagement," where they are more intrinsically motivated to learn.[2] But how do we get there? The following questions can help guide the way.

Is this challenging? Sometimes students check out because they find the work too easy. We can solve this by creating meaningful enrichment activities for students who want to take their learning to the next level.

Are students engaged in critical thinking? Are students just absorbing information only to later regurgitate it on a test? Or are they poking and prodding it, exploring information from different angles and reaching different outcomes? Students need to engage in analysis, synthesis, and creative thinking. When this happens, they're more likely to get excited about the learning.

How can I make this relevant? Students want to explore their world and pursue their interests. I know a teacher who wanted her third-grade class to learn a little about the war that was just beginning in Ukraine. It was massive news and she wanted her students to have a basic understanding of the conflict. It also connected with third-grade social studies content standards. She knew most of her students would be unable to relate to or even connect with such a huge and distant global conflict. So she had her students focus on the zoo animals that were affected by the conflict by learning about and raising funds for the zoos that were hurt by the war.

This teacher knows that most third graders love animals and would empathize with those that are in trouble. Zoo animals were relevant to her students. By tapping into this relevancy, her students were now more open to learning the content of class and understanding the broader subject of this learning unit.

Is there any creativity? Inherent with creativity is an element of novelty and surprise. When students are not just solving problems or uncovering information, but instead are creating something new, their brains are activated in dynamic ways. Neurotransmitters like dopamine and serotonin are released within the brain. Dopamine, associated with pleasure and reward, can enhance motivation and focus, driving the creator to persist in their creative endeavors. Serotonin, linked to mood and well-being, can influence the overall positive experience of creating.

During the act of creation, students engage in divergent thinking, where their brains are activated in more than one way to solve problems. They exercise their basal ganglia, a part of the brain that acts as the control center. And each time we create, we strengthen it, allowing for smoother execution of ideas as a creator gains expertise.

So whether it is as simple as adding a small element of creativity to every lesson, whether it's a short writing prompt or having students sketch their learning, or whether it's converting an entire learning unit to a project where students are creating a solution to a major problem, creativity should play a central role in your curriculum.

Problem #2: Students Are Antsy and Impatient

There's a different type of boredom that has less to do with boredom and more to do with general restlessness. Here, students are antsy and impatient. They might be staring off at nothing or tipping their chairs or passing notes. They might be sneaking peeks at their Snapchat or doodling comic book pictures in the margins of the textbook. This is often a sign of a pacing problem. We're moving too slowly through a task and they're ready to move on to something different.

The Solution: Change Up the Pace

Sometimes you need to cancel the current task and switch to something new. This can be especially hard because we often design tasks and activities with the thought that they are going to be effective, only to be met with eye rolls, pencil tapping, and Minecraft underneath the desk. Letting go of preconceived expectations can be difficult and require that we swallow our pride. Sometimes we need to accept that an activity is not working. Whether it's because of the activity itself, the way we delivered it, or there's a full moon that day and students have lost their minds, it's okay to sometimes abandon ship and try something else.

However, there are moments when the lesson is well crafted and you need students to stay focused. In these moments, you can break it up with a quick two-minute brain break or divergent thinking activity. Other times, you might want to do a quick collaboration activity. Sometimes, students simply need a quick think-pair-share to process what they're learning.

As a more preventative approach, you can focus your lesson planning on varying the grouping so that students have time to work individually, discuss ideas with a partner, and engage in group work. Some students are really more social and simply need the opportunity to talk.

I remember saying to a teacher-friend, "I have a really chatty group of students this year," and he responded with "How often are they getting the chance to talk to one another?" When I analyzed my lesson, I realized students were only getting the chance to talk about 10% of the time. So, I redesigned it to incorporate more peer and group discourse, and then, when I did direct instruction, I would say, "I need 10 minutes of your time and then you'll have the chance to talk." It made a huge difference.

Problem #3: Students Are Confused

Have you ever given directions to students only to face a class of glossy-eyed students and a sea of raised hands minutes later? Yeah, us too. I can't count the number of times when students got off-task because they were confused about what they were supposed to do.

Solution: Redesign with Clarity

Sometimes you need to remind students of the classroom procedures. If you've created a procedure chart, this is a chance to review it. However, other times, the issue involves a lack of clarity in assignment directions or lesson materials. These are the moments when you can redesign an assignment, change a procedure, or fix a system that's unclear in your classroom. We'll take a deeper dive into this topic in Chapter 5.

Problem #4: Students Don't Respect My Authority

I can't count the number of times someone told me, "Remember that you're the teacher, not their friend." And yet, in my first year of teaching, I found myself slipping into the "friend" role with my sixth-hour class. They were the honor's group and they seemed to naturally follow the rules without much prompting. So, I started acting more like a peer. I let small disruptions go unchecked because I relished my status as the "cool teacher." Then something happened. The class grew more and more disruptive and they didn't listen to me when I corrected them.

Solution: Set Healthy Boundaries

There needs to be clear boundaries between you and your students. While still in relationship with them, students need to know that that relationship is not a peer one.

- **Clearly communicate roles and expectations.** Discuss and educate students on appropriate teacher-student boundaries at the beginning of the school year. Emphasize the importance of maintaining a respectful and professional relationship.

- **Maintain professionalism.** Demonstrate professionalism in all interactions with students. Refrain from using offensive language, inappropriate jokes, or any language that may be disrespectful or offensive to students. This is not always easy, especially as you become more comfortable with your students, but while humor should be encouraged in the classroom, it cannot be at the expense of any of your students' dignity and well-being.

- **Avoid sharing personal information unnecessarily.** While being vulnerable and open with your students is important, we still need to refrain from oversharing personal details or experiences. Students do need to know their teachers are human, but they do not need every intimate detail from your life. This can lead to misinterpretation, inappropriate assumptions, and difficulty to regain professional boundaries once personal information has been shared.

- **Keep physical boundaries.** Be mindful of physical boundaries by maintaining appropriate physical distance and avoiding unnecessary physical contact with students. Even if your intentions are perfectly innocent, physical touch can be misconstrued and misinterpreted. It is better to affirm students in other ways, and avoid physical contact for your sake and theirs.

- **Be consistent in discipline and rules.** Apply classroom rules and disciplinary actions consistently and fairly to all students. Avoid favoritism or biased treatment that may blur the boundaries of the teacher-student relationship.

- **Set appropriate communication channels.** Use school email or your school's designated communication apps to communicate with students. It might be more convenient to give students your cell phone number, but this can lead to a whole host of problems. At its simplest, you might receive annoying texts at night or on the weekend. More seriously, it can violate the boundaries between you and your students.

- **Be mindful of online interactions.** Your school may or may not have a policy on whether teachers can engage with students on social media, but as a general rule, it is usually best to avoid those online interactions. If you use social media, it is most likely where you share personal details about your life with people you are connected with. You may not want your students to have access to all of those details, and you also may not want to see the details from your students' lives. I (Trevor) have always told my students that they can follow me on social media after they graduate. Until then, all friend and follow requests will receive a hard "NO."

Listen, all those veteran teachers were right. You're not their friend. You're their teacher, which is better than being a friend. You're the architect designing epic lessons. You're the mentor guiding them. You're the stable adult listening to them when they share something that breaks your heart. Maintaining professional boundaries with students does not lessen your relationship with them; instead, it enhances it.

Problem #5: Students Are Simply Struggling with the Work

Sometimes negative student behavior is simply students communicating that they are struggling with the task you assign them. Of course, the work you give to students should be challenging, but a common reaction to challenging work is often frustration, apathy, or disruptive behavior. It's the student putting their head down and opting for a nap instead of another math problem. It's flinging a book on the ground, crossing their arms, and refusing to read a passage from a book. It's throwing pencils across the room or blurting out when the room is supposed to be quiet. Often, the root of this type of behavior can be found in the work we assign students.

Solution: Improve Scaffolding

Scaffolding is a teaching and learning strategy that involves providing support, guidance, and structure to students as they develop new skills or understanding in a particular subject. This support is tailored to the learner's abilities and gradually reduced as the student becomes more proficient and self-sufficient in their learning.

We need to provide meaningful scaffolds for our students. This might include sentence stems, tutorials, templates, anchor charts, and exemplars. It requires viewing learning as a process. While this can feel daunting for teachers, it can help to ask students to self-select the scaffolding. Other times, you might want to modify the quantity of the work.

In education, we tend to place a high premium on getting the right answer and getting it quickly. Students internalize a fixed mindset, convinced that they are bad at the subject simply because it takes them longer to finish. However, when we allow students to work at a slower pace, and provide intentional guidance along the way, they don't feel as overwhelmed by the sense that they are always behind. And as a result, their behavior often adjusts accordingly.

Tackling Challenging Behaviors

It can help to think about behavior as a before, during, and after approach. As you think about an incident, ask, "What could I do beforehand to prevent this?" Next, reflect on what you are doing during that incident and consider what you might do in the moment. Then, think about how you will address the incident afterward with students.

Incident	Before	During	After
Students are talking while the teacher is giving directions.	Teach a hand signal for getting the class's attention. Make sure the directions are clear and that there are visuals to go with it. If the directions have multiple steps, explain one step and have students explain it to a partner. Then move to the next step. This can help reduce cognitive load.	Stand up straight. Take a deep breath. Give the students eye contact, and quietly walk over to their table. If the talking persists, quietly ask them to stop. Continue giving the directions from the location of table.	As students work in groups, ask the students who are talking, "What were you supposed to be doing? What will you do differently next time?" Note that you don't need to have a formal consequence. This can be a learning experience.

It Takes Years to Master

Heather Schanski is a first-grade teacher of 26 years. She's taught both of my (Trevor) kids, and I've had the opportunity to observe her teach many times.

I don't say this lightly: Heather is a master teacher. One of the best I've ever witnessed. I asked her if she could sum up her classroom management plan in a paragraph, and this is what she said:

Even after teaching for many years, there is one area that is challenging every year, and that is classroom management. What works smoothly for one group may not work with another. A technique can even work for every student in a class, with the exception of one! For me, I look at classroom management similarly to teaching a complex standard. Not all students learn the same way. One child may need to be taught many different ways. Behavior is just like that. But one thing always rings true. Relationships and trust make a classroom! Spend the time from day one engaging, connecting, and caring for each and every student. Those genuine connections alone will pay great dividends for positive behavior.

As the father of two kids who learned to read, write, and love learning from Heather, I can confirm the efficacy of the connection between the relationships she builds with students and the way they engage in her class. Her students adore her, and as a result, thrive in her classroom.

Heather is a treasure.

But I'm also struck by her admission that managing students is still a challenge. Even after 26 years, perfection remains elusive. Classroom management is a craft that takes years to master—and even then, it will still be challenging.

Process this fact. Internalize it. Adopt it into your new teacher mindset.

And then have copious amounts of grace for yourself as you move forward. Expecting every strategy to be successful or every student to respond to you with engagement and respect is not possible. You will grow in your ability to maintain student engagement, possibly even become a master in that ability, but you'll never be perfect at it.

And that's perfectly okay.

Notes

1. Tze, V.M.C., Daniels, L. M., and Klassen, R. M. (2016). Evaluating the relationship between boredom and academic outcomes: A meta-analysis. *Educational Psychology Review, 28*, 119–144. https://doi.org/10.1007/s10648-015-9301-y
2. Schlechty, P. C. (2002). *Working on the work: An action plan for teachers, principals, and superintendents.* The Jossey-Bass Education Series. Jossey-Bass.

Nurturing an Ecosystem Students Actually Want to Learn In

I (Trevor) moved to a new school in my fifth year as a teacher. By this time in my career, I felt like I was finally getting the hang of being a teacher and was eager to make a splash at this new school I was joining. When I arrived, I wanted to be loved. I wanted students to like my class, and if I'm being honest, I wanted word to get out to my principal and make him feel ecstatic in his decision to hire me.

So on the first day of school, and I cringe a little bit sharing this, I was like a crazy man. I approached that first week of school as if I was a stand-up comedian. My chief goal was to make my students feel like when you're in Mr. Muir's English class, you are always going to have fun. I was standing up on tables and rapping to Eminem songs. I hung up a basketball hoop on the door; I looked the other way when kids were playing Minecraft on their computers. I did everything in my power to make my class fun and entertaining.

If I could make all of my students love being in my class, engaging them in lessons and projects would come easily. Because they loved being with me, they would listen and respect me. And it worked! Students really did look forward to coming to my class, and I was getting the reputation as a fun teacher.

And I'll be honest, I really liked that.

I liked seeing kids smile when they came into my classroom. Nothing feels quite as amazing as being called a student's "favorite teacher." And if I'm being honest, I loved knowing that this reputation was growing and that even parents were telling my principal how much their kids loved their new English teacher.

The Problem with This Reputation

However, always present in the back of my mind was this frustration that students were not taking me seriously. It took 10 minutes every class period to calm them down enough to start the lesson, leaving 45 minutes for the rest of class. Some students would take the bathroom pass and disappear for the rest of the period. Silent reading was nearly impossible, assignments were not submitted, and chaos ensued on a regular basis. It also didn't help that most of my students were scoring poor grades in my class.

One day I was out sick, and I came back to a note from the substitute that wrote in all capital letters that YOUR CLASS WAS OUT OF CONTROL! GET CONTROL OF THESE KIDS! THEY MADE ME CRY!

I realized that this wasn't love; this was disrespect. So one day, I pulled one of the students whom I was having trouble with, a ringleader of sorts, into the hallway and leveled with him. I said, "Why are you guys acting like this?"

He looked at me and replied, "Because you acted crazy at the beginning of the year. You were standing on tables and didn't care if the class got loud. I thought you were cool with it."

And I didn't know how to respond because he was right.

Building a Strong Foundation

My class had a climate problem, and it was evident that it was rooted in the tone I set as a teacher. As we covered in the previous chapter, we should absolutely smile before Christmas and share joy with students starting on day one. However, I was quickly learning that "fun" is not a strong enough foundation for a thriving classroom. A positive classroom climate must go beyond fun into something deeper—a place where students thrive as they engage in authentic learning.

It's kind of like the difference between weather and climate. Weather is the result of the climate. Of course I want fun to happen in the classroom, but that should be a result of the overall climate. The classroom needs a positive atmosphere for students to comfortably work, learn, and create. This is the classroom climate. We want students to walk into a space and feel known and respected. We want to cultivate a positive classroom climate, but this positive space won't always be fun or goofy or entertaining. It will also be challenging and contentious. It will vary between noisy laughter, intense discussions, and silent focus.

Creating a Positive Climate

As a university professor, I (John) have spent years in countless classrooms doing observations. Whether it's a group of eager-eyed kindergarteners or confident seniors in an AP Government class, I can sense the climate within minutes. What does it feel like to inhabit this space? What is the emotional pulse of the classroom? What's the overall atmosphere?

While classroom culture and classroom climate are closely related, we define *climate* as the way a space feels, while *culture* is more about how a classroom defines itself (its identity, values, and norms). We'll explore this idea of culture in the next chapter.

In thinking about climate, driving questions might include: "Is there an atmosphere of mutual respect? Do students feel a sense of belonging? Do they feel the freedom to contribute ideas and work collaboratively? Do they feel the permission to challenge ideas?"

The goal of a positive classroom climate is to design a space where students experience a sense of belonging.

If the answer is "yes," then it's likely a positive classroom climate.

A positive climate doesn't need to be saccharine. You don't need to hang motivational posters with a photograph and a single word like *Perseverance* underneath. It should, however, feel inviting and warm. Students should walk in with the sense that you are glad to see them.

Furthermore, a positive climate is not necessarily happy all the time. Some of the most positive classroom climates include moments of conflict and healthy frustration. They're spaces where students and teachers feel the freedom to express their emotions. Here, *positive* doesn't mean everyone is in a great mood all the time. Instead, it is an environment where students express their emotions in a way that is kind and respectful. In other words, a positive climate is less about the mood and more about the mindset of looking for solutions.

Similarly, a positive climate isn't necessarily focused on pleasant topics. It doesn't mean ignoring injustice or only teaching the happy incidents in history. It doesn't involve reading only happy stories in language arts. A positive mindset asks students to wade into the discomfort as they tackle issues like racism and sexism. Even if students feel uncomfortable in the moment as they explore racial biases, the ultimate goal is positive—helping students grow as people.

In thinking about a positive classroom climate, it can help to consider the difference between positive spaces and toxic positivity. Therapist Whitney Goodman views toxic positivity as a form of gaslighting, where people do not have the permission to experience negative emotions like anger or sadness.[1] These toxically positive climates require people to stay upbeat no matter what, even going so far as having to smile even when experiencing pain. These climates convey an upbeat and cheerful picture of the world while pushing away negative content, thoughts, or discussions. Toxic positivity can lead to shame, guilt, and insecurity.

In genuinely positive spaces, individuals can express themselves authentically, seek genuine support, and work through challenges while acknowledging a full range of emotions. On the other hand, toxic positivity suppresses valid emotions, dismisses problems, and can lead to invalidation of individuals' experiences. Balancing positivity with a realistic understanding of challenges and emotions is key to fostering a truly supportive and growth-oriented environment. The following chart explores these differences.

Positivity Versus Toxic Positivity

Aspect	Positive Spaces	Toxic Positive Spaces
Emotional Range	Embraces a wide range of emotions as valid with the ultimate goal of permission.	Invalidates negative emotions as "bad."
Authenticity	Encourages authentic expression and vulnerability.	Suppresses true feelings for the sake of appearing positive.
Support	Provides genuine support and empathy. Understands that a positive outcome can sometimes involve unpleasant conversations.	Offers dismissive phrases without understanding.
Problem-Solving	Focuses on addressing issues constructively.	Avoids acknowledging problems altogether.
Criticism	Accepts constructive criticism for growth. Sees constructive criticism as an ultimately positive endeavor.	Rejects criticism as it's seen as "negativity."

Aspect	Positive Spaces	Toxic Positive Spaces
Toxic Behaviors	Does not tolerate toxic behavior or bullying.	Masks harmful behavior in the name of being positive. Avoids addressing these behaviors by distracting people with fun.
Personal Growth	Values personal growth and learning.	Assumes one should always be happy and growth is automatic.
Resilience	Encourages resilience through challenges. Offers the permission to make mistakes and grow.	Pressure to quickly "get over" difficulties. Sometimes lowers the standards to make sure no one has to fail.
Empathy	Cultivates empathy and understanding.	Empathy is lacking due to focus on forced positivity.
Self-Compassion	Supports being kind to oneself in struggles.	Views self-care as selfish or indulgent.
Communication	Fosters open and honest communication.	Promotes surface-level, shallow positivity.
Mental Health	Prioritizes mental health and well-being.	Ignores mental health challenges or stigmatizes them.

Characteristics of a Positive Classroom Climate

A positive classroom climate can be defined by four key Markers. As we explore these Markers, consider your own classroom experiences. Which classrooms had these characteristics? What was it like for you as a student? Let's start with joy.

Marker #1: Creating a Climate of Joy

"Dream big. There are no bad ideas. We can make things possible later," I (John) told students as they began a classroom redesign project. It was part of a STEAM project that would ultimately lead to our first-ever makerspace.

Students drew inspiration from coffee shops, libraries, fast-food joints, museums, and skate parks. However, a few students embraced the "dream big" idea to the ultimate extent and asked for a roller coaster. At that moment, I asked, "How can we make this happen? It's too expensive, too dangerous, and too big."

Perhaps the "dream big" idea had backfired. But then I had an idea. It was goofy but it might just work. I took a drink coaster and some duct tape, and I combined these with a little wheel from a LEGO® set. We ended up with a coaster that you can roll back and forth. Hence, a roller coaster. I created three more roller coasters.

When students arrived, I said, "We have four functioning roller coasters in class for our redesign."

Was it a really bad example of prop humor? Absolutely.

Did it work? Most definitely. This goofy joke grew into something bigger. Students started to brag about the roller coasters. I walked into the staff lounge and a teacher asked, "Is it true that you have a roller coaster?"

"Yep," I answered.

"Like a real one? A functional roller coaster?"

"Yes," I said. "We actually have four of them."

Parents who had never emailed me before asked if their kids had lied to them.

Students would tell their younger siblings before student-teacher conferences, "You need to check out the roller coasters."

This became a part of our classroom culture. It was an inside joke that helped create a positive climate. Humor, goofiness, joy, fun—these are actually vital to developing a positive classroom culture.

At first, I thought of this as comic relief. This was the icing on the cake. I secretly wondered if I was getting away with something. But eventually, I realized that this was a critical aspect of a positive culture. There's something very serious about silliness.

Humor Creates Psychological Safety　　There's a reason epic stories use comic relief. By engaging in humor, the author creates an "up" that allows the reader to delve deeper into something darker or more tense. Think of the *Harry Potter* series. J.K. Rowling's use of humor (especially in the first few books) allowed the books to delve into some darker topics as they faced Vold . . . er . . . I mean, "he who must not be named."

The same is true in schools. We sometimes touch on some hard topics and once we've laughed together, we are more likely to be comfortable with hard conversations. Psychologists have demonstrated that humor can lead to psychological safety. Humor creates a sense of levity that puts everyone at ease. When this happens, team members are more open-minded, more willing to offer alternative perspectives, and better able to engage in creative risk-taking. Which leads to the next point. . . .

Humor Encourages Creative Risk-Taking   There is a vulnerability to humor because, whether we want to admit it or not, we are trying to be humorous . . . or at least witty each time we attempt humor. It's a small element of risk-taking.

When I taught middle school, we had a wordplay wall at the back with ridiculously bad dad jokes (things like "fire drill" and "slow jams" and "graduated cylinder"). We had Easter eggs hidden throughout the classroom.

And the truth is, many of my students rolled their eyes at this. They said things like, "Ugh, dad jokes!"

But something else happened. Some students started drawing their own pun jokes, like "Reese's Peanut Butter Cop" a cartoon chocolate in a police outfit.

It gave students permission to be goofy and nerdy and whimsical. And in the process, it gave people permission to have their own unique creative voice. This quirkiness infused the entire classroom culture. Students internalized an unspoken message that it's okay to be different. In fact, that's precisely what makes them awesome.

Humor Boosts Creative Problem-Solving   Dr. Karuna Subramaniam ran a research study at Northwestern University where people watched various genres of videos.[2] She then had participants engage in problem-solving tasks, word associations (convergent thinking), and brainstorming (divergent thinking) afterward. She found that those who watched comedy videos scored better in every area of creative problem-solving than those who watched horror or a lecture on quantum electronics. In another study, researcher Barry Kudrowitz demonstrated that improvisational humor increases ideation because of the transferable skill of relating to seemingly unrelated ideas.[3]

Humor creates a lightened mood and a mental spaciousness that makes it easier to engage in connective thinking. We embrace a playful mindset where we are more open to new ideas and primed to engage in flexible thinking.

Humor Should Always Be Kind Humor is deeply personal and idiosyncratic. Each person's cultural background, media consumption, personal histories, family experiences, and personality play a role in shaping what we find funny. Your humor has to come from who you are. I know a teacher who makes her students laugh with her dry humor and flat delivery. She's calm and her smile is so subtle you might mistake it for a smirk. But she models creative risk-taking and has a classroom environment where students feel safe laughing. I know of another teacher who dresses up in costumes, who will engage in an impromptu dance-off, and whose humor is physical and over-the-top—and his students loved being in that space. Both of these fourth-grade teachers allow their students to embrace humor and joy as well—and you can sense this joy the moment you step into their classrooms.

In both cases, though, the humor came from a place of kindness. Humor is a powerful tool, but that tool can be used to cause irreparable damage. As teachers, we need to set parameters around humor. For example, you might set a rule that humor should never be aimed at an individual or a group of people. So, name-calling would be off-limits. At an older age, you might explain the difference between irony, sarcasm, and cynicism.

At some point, humor can become a distraction as well. Excessive humor and off-topic stories can pull students away from valuable learning time and make the content harder to understand. But when used well, humor can create a more positive classroom climate.

How Do We Do This? Here are a few ideas for infusing humor into your classroom.

1. **Create a collection of memes that you can integrate into your lessons.** You can use humorous memes as a way to do a quick emotional pulse check. You can also integrate the memes into a warm-up before a particular lesson.

2. **Find the goofy jokes within content areas.** These might be science jokes (don't trust atoms, they make up everything) or math jokes (the problem with 90-degree angles is they have to be right all the time). You might display these on the board or if you're feeling particularly nerdy, you might wear a joke on a T-shirt (like the "pi-rate" shirt I wear on March 17 every year). The idea is to get students to see that there's a sense of playfulness even in challenging subject areas.

3. **Create a set of inside jokes within your class.** Some of the best comedians use "call back" lines where they allude to an earlier part of their set. Similarly, in a classroom, inside jokes can have a "call back" effect that leads to more and more layers within the joke. These inside jokes help create a more cohesive community as well.

4. **Keep track of funny stories.** By paying attention to the humorous events around us, we can infuse our lessons with small examples of funny stories that then lead to higher student engagement.

5. **Use props and visual puns.** You don't have to go full-scale Carrot Top here. But the idea is that certain prop humor of puns can work really well with certain age groups. This is especially true with silly props in early elementary levels.

Marker #2: Creating a Climate of Wonder

Earlier I (John) mentioned the classroom redesign project where we began planning for a makerspace. While the initial project was successful, as we began deciding on key items we needed for the space, I mistakenly shifted my focus from the *maker* to the *space*. I fixated on key items I thought we needed, and I felt defeated when we couldn't purchase certain expensive equipment. I had this dream of the perfect space with the nicest furniture and the top-of-the-line, high-tech gadgetry, and I knew we would never afford this in our underfunded Title I school.

Then I thought about the role of classroom climate. A makerspace is only a makerspace because it inspires students to be creative. I started thinking about the creative classroom spaces I had visited before. The theater room. The music room. The art room. The woodshop class. These were all makerspaces. But so was that amazing math class where students debated strategies and sketched out their ideas on a room full of whiteboards. So was that language arts classroom where students were immersed in various novels and where they crafted their own blog posts and essays.

Every class can be a makerspace.

At the top of my makerspace planning document, I wrote the words "This classroom should be a bastion of creativity and wonder."

I wanted students to walk in and find something that would spark their curiosity and inspire problem-solving. Some of this would involve the physical space (an idea we will explore in a future chapter), but so much of this would involve the general climate of the space. It would occur in conversations and interactive activities.

In math, it might look like a design sprint, where students have to find the correct number of arrays for a solar farm. Students eagerly explore patterns, ask questions, and look for creative approaches to solve the challenge. Here, they compare and contrast strategies.

In reading, wonder takes the form of enthusiastic discussions about characters' motives and predicting plot twists, driven by a genuine interest in uncovering the layers of a story. Other times, it might involve asking a research question for a Wonder Day project and then engaging in a deep-dive lateral reading with multiple sources before ultimately sharing their answer in a blog post or podcast. We can watch the curiosity ignite as students explore diverse topics and experiment with different styles, driven by a desire to express themselves and communicate effectively.

In a PE class, we can observe students' curiosity as they explore their physical capabilities, try new activities, and ask questions about the body's mechanics and nutrition. We see it in their goal-setting activities and their self-reflections.

Curiosity is at the heart of science. It's what drives the entire inquiry process as students question the natural world, conduct experiments, and hypothesize about the "why" and "how" of phenomena. Some of my favorite science teachers have students engaged in frequent state of wonder that borders on confusion. But this increased curiosity helps students persevere and engage in productive struggle (an idea we'll explore in the next Marker). Across all these subjects, wonder and curiosity propel students to actively seek knowledge, expand their perspectives, and develop a lifelong love of learning.

Marker #3: Creating a Climate Where Students Struggle

Halfway through the school year, I had students do a climate survey about the makerspace. Many of the students described the sense of fun and enjoyment from solving problems and engaging in projects. But a surprising trend also occurred: the number of students who described the struggles they had experienced.

In a survey, one student described it perfectly. "This is a fun space but sometimes it's not. It's also a place where I play with ideas and ask questions. It's a place where I am challenged to think deeply. Sometimes I get stuck, and I get frustrated and I even get angry. So, even though this space is fun, I'm not always having fun. Does that make sense?" It made perfect sense to me.

When we create a climate of wonder, we open up students for productive struggle. Here, they engage in challenging tasks that often push them mentally and even psychologically. This struggle requires extra effort, critical thinking, and, ultimately, perseverance. It is a constructive approach to problem-solving, where students actively grapple with difficulties rather than avoiding them. In this type of climate, students have the permission to make mistakes and to grow. They move through multiple interactions as they attempt to solve a challenging problem. As educators, we are providing students with slack so they can develop grit.

Like the student described in the survey, productive struggle isn't always fun. But it is positive. Students may experience moments of frustration or uncertainty, but these moments are seen as valuable opportunities for growth. Through persistent effort, they learn from mistakes. Along the way, they experience a sense of empowerment as they navigate complex challenges in new ways.

Ways to Encourage Productive Struggle:

1. **Ask open-ended questions**. Pose questions that don't have immediate answers. This encourages students to explore different approaches and solutions. Note that these questions don't have to be abstract. They can be concrete, but also the kind that leads to additional questions.

2. **Assign challenging tasks**. Assign tasks slightly above students' current skill levels. This encourages them to stretch their abilities and think creatively to

overcome challenges. Researchers have noted that students are most likely to hit a state of flow when the task is just above their skill level (or even their perceived skill level). It's what makes video games so addicting!

3. **Avoid giving immediate help.** Tell students that there will be a 5- to 10-minute period where they need to work on a challenging problem, and you will not provide any help.

4. **Provide feedback, not answers.** Instead of providing direct answers, offer feedback that guides students' thinking and redirects them when they encounter obstacles.

5. **Keep it ungraded.** Part of why students get anxious about productive struggle is the feeling that this might lead to a lower grade. For this reason, you can keep the task ungraded or allow multiple submissions.

6. **Celebrate "epic fails" as a class.** Have students share their epic fail with a partner and then do share alouds where students reveal what mistake they made, what they learned, and what they plan to do differently next time.

7. **Implement scaffolded learning.** Sometimes students struggle because they are hitting cognitive overload. This is often considered "extraneous cognitive load." You can break down complex tasks into smaller, manageable steps. As students progress through each step, they build confidence and tackle the larger challenge. Offer a variety of resources like books, articles, videos, and experts to help students explore different aspects of a topic and develop a deeper understanding. This will allow students to experience productive struggle in a way that is manageable.

8. **Walk through the emotions of productive struggle.** Create moments of reflection for students that allow students to explore the natural emotions they might experience as they struggle. Remember that a positive climate sometimes has frustration, disappointment, and even anger.

9. **Give examples of productive struggle.** Share stories of famous individuals who faced challenges and setbacks but eventually achieved success through determination and effort. Show students examples of their favorite shows, products, and works of art that required multiple iterations.

Marker #4: Creating a Climate of Belonging

I (Trevor) once had a principal who did not trust me and seemingly questioned every move I made in the classroom. It wasn't long under their leadership before I stopped making those moves. I quit dressing up in costumes when teaching history lessons for fear of being labeled as "unprofessional" by my boss. I scaled down the scope of the projects I did with students because I feared something would go wrong and I would face punishment. I no longer brought in guest speakers to my class because I couldn't control every word they said, and my principal made it clear that teachers should control every word said to students.

I lost confidence in myself as a teacher, and as a result, became a worse one. This ended in me leaving that school and going somewhere I could be confident again.

The same is true for students. If they are forced to work and engage in a strained climate that is dictated more by fear than trust, this will affect their confidence and quality of work in class. Except students usually do not have the option to find a better school and teacher.

At a core level, a positive climate includes a sense of safety, where students know that they have a place of belonging. The term *safe space* has been hotly debated and politicized in recent years. There's a perception that psychological safety means students won't be exposed to uncomfortable ideas or philosophies they disagree with. However, professor and organizational psychologist Adam Grant makes an important distinction, "Don't confuse psychological safety with 'safe spaces.' Safe spaces treat people as fragile and dissenting ideas as threats. Psychologically safe environments build the capacity to embrace and learn from respectful disagreement. Exposure to diverging views is fuel for growth."[4]

Timothy R. Clark describes psychological safety as a set of stages beginning with the overall sense of belonging and moving toward a place where people have the freedom to challenge ideas.[5] He conceptualizes it in four stages. And while he focuses on organizations led by adults, we'd like to share what this might mean for students.

1. **Inclusion:** In this initial stage, students feel a sense of belonging and acceptance by their immediate team and the class as a whole. They perceive that their contributions are valued, even if it's at an initially shallower level. Overall,

they feel like they can be themselves within the larger classroom community because the students and the teacher treat each other with respect, fostering a sense of mutual dignity.

2. **Learner safety:** In this stage, students feel comfortable expressing their thoughts, ideas, and even mistakes without fearing negative consequences. They believe that asking questions, seeking feedback, and admitting lack of knowledge are welcomed and encouraged. Students are encouraged to express their thoughts, questions, and opinions without fear of judgment. Teachers encourage constructive and open dialogue, and students thus feel the freedom to admit when they don't know the answer.

3. **Contributor safety:** As psychological safety deepens, students actively contribute their ideas, opinions, and skills without apprehension. They are confident that their input will be considered constructively, even if it challenges the status quo or diverges from the majority. As teachers, we can build interdependence into our lessons so that each student can contribute to the learning. Whether it's a deeper collaboration or a simple cooperative learning activity, students know they are contributing to the larger learning environment. In some cases, teachers might even have classroom jobs for students.

4. **Challenger safety:** At the highest level of psychological safety, individuals feel empowered to challenge assumptions, propose innovative solutions, and engage in open and constructive debates. They know that expressing dissenting viewpoints is not only allowed but also valued for fostering growth and better decision-making within the group. The classroom embraces a diverse range of backgrounds, perspectives, and experiences, creating a sense of belonging for all students. They understand that conflict is a natural part of intellectual diversity and they don't shy away from it.

These stages reflect a progression toward a work environment where individuals can truly be themselves, express their thoughts without fear, and engage in meaningful interactions that lead to innovation and collaboration.

The following are some guiding questions you might ask yourself about the sense of belonging students feel in your classroom:

- Do students from all cultural backgrounds see themselves in the classroom climate?
- Is this a climate that embraces neurodiversity?
- Is this a climate that allows introverted and extroverted students to thrive?
- Do students from marginalized groups have a voice in this space?
- Is this a safe space for LGBT+ students?
- Do students feel the permission to make mistakes in this class?
- Does every students have a role or job in what we are doing?
- What elements of the climate encourage or discourage students from offering a dissenting viewpoint?

Affirming Introverts and Extroverts   If we want to cultivate a sense of belonging in our classroom climate, we need to ensure that the climate is affirming to both introverted and extroverted students. As a student, I (John) sometimes felt ignored and alone as an introvert. I grew overwhelmed by the noise and chaos of a classroom environment. I wanted a space where I could decompress. By contrast, I (Trevor) was often sent to the office for being overly social and talkative during independent work or in the midst of a longer segment of direct instruction.

All too often introverts get ignored while extroverts get in trouble.

So, how do we change this in our classroom climate? One idea is to vary the internal and external processing time for students. Start each class period with a silent warm-up. You might start out with deliberate silence, like a journaling activity, a sketch-note session, or a mindfulness activity. But it might simply be a chance to plan out the project, complete a related question, or engage in a free-write.

However, this initial moment of silence can help introverts relax and re-center themselves before entering into a collaborative project. Afterward, give students the chance to do a pair-share where they interact with one another. This will honor both introverts and extroverts.

In a math exercise, you might have students working alone on a single problem, but then you can create a break after five minutes to allow students to compare and contrast strategies or to teach a new concept to one another. They might work out an idea on paper followed by a highly interactive whiteboard activity where a whole group tries to solve the problem together.

If you're doing a class discussion, you might create two separate discussion models. The first would be an open-ended, highly interactive Socratic Seminar. The second option might be a digital backchannel, where students engage in a synchronous discussion where they type out their answers quietly. They might even prefer an asynchronous option like a forum or discussion board. Students then get to decide which type of space they want to inhabit.

Making Sure Students Feel Affirmed   An inclusive classroom climate is ultimately affirming to all students at the group level. However, we can also make intentional efforts to affirm each student at an individual level.

Six Ways to Affirm Students

1. **Praise publicly and critique privately.** Public corrections often lead to students being more risk-averse. When we correct a behavior, it can lead to power struggles as students try to save face. So this means you avoid saying, "Student A, I need you to stop talking," and instead publicly praise a group of students who are following the class norms.

2. **Affirm each student at least once per week.** Keep track of the number of times you affirm each student, using their seating chart as a starting point. It might be as simple as saying, "Aiden, thanks for getting back to your table quickly." You might acknowledge a student's effort in solving a challenging problem.

3. **Send positive notes home on a schedule.** If you take notes on what students are doing well, you can convert these notes into a physical note home or an

email. It is easy to fall into the trap of contacting caregivers only when a student is acting up. But when you affirm each child in a positive email home, that can have a profound effect on your relationship with the student and their parent or guardian.

4. **Create birthday celebrations.** I used to print my own birthday cards. They were simple and low-budget. I also bought individual candy bars based on the survey students filled out the first day of school. Then, on their birthday, we would sing "Happy Birthday" and they got a card with their favorite candy bar. While it's true that some students don't celebrate birthdays, you can create a separate nonbirthday celebration for that student instead.

5. **Learn about extracurricular activities or interests outside of school.** Ask students about the activities as they walk into school.

6. **Have students engage in structured peer affirmations.** Have each student fill out an anonymous Google Form with every student's name on it. Then let them submit a positive affirmation. You can collect it as a list and create a word cloud to go with it.

It Won't Be Perfect   A few years ago, a former student reached out to me (John) for advice on cultivating a positive classroom climate. As a pre-service teacher, she was about to enter her student teaching experience.

"Any practical ideas for things I can do to keep the climate positive?"

"I don't know. I made a lot of mistakes with your group. I was a new teacher. I remember getting impatient with your class at times."

"I guess so, but that's not really what I remember," she said. She then described her favorite moments of that year. We laughed at some of the stories she recalled.

"I'm glad that's how you remember it. I still cringe sometimes at the mistakes I made. I would love to do it over again knowing what I know now."

"Well, I remember feeling safe in that classroom. Safe but also challenged. I loved being in your class."

I learned from this interaction the difference between weather and climate. My impatience, frustration, and mistakes were rainy days. *They were weather*. Weather doesn't define the climate. Climate is about the overall pattern, and this former student said the pattern she remembers was one of warmth.

Notes

1. Harrington, Kimberly. (2022). What is "toxic positivity" and why is it a problem? A new book explains. https://www.washingtonpost.com/books/2022/01/27/toxic-positivity-book/
2. Subramaniam, K. (2018, October 2). Title of the work [Dissertation]. Neuroscience Institute Graduate Program. https://doi.org/10.21985/N28Q88
3. University of Minnesota. (n.d.). What humor & creativity can teach us about innovation. Retrieved from https://clinicalaffairs.umn.edu/news/what-humor-creativity-can-teach-us-about-innovation
4. Grant, A. (2022, January 14). [Tweet]. Twitter. https://x.com/AdamMGrant/status/1695452949583888738?s=20
5. Clark, T. R. (2020). *The stages of psychological safety: Defining the path to inclusion and innovation.* Berrett-Koehler Publishers.

Classroom Culture and Unifying Your Students

On the first day of every school year, I (Trevor) always start class with "Good Thing," first playing a snippet of the song, "Tell Me Something Good," and then give students three seconds each to share something good or positive that's happening in their lives. Common responses include: "I won my soccer game last night," "It's my mom's birthday" (kids love to tell you when it's their mom's birthday), "I ate waffles for breakfast," or "I won Fortnite last night."

And then on the second day of the school year, I do this again. When we have exams, I start class with "Good Things." On the day before the holiday break, we start class this way. When there's a school assembly and shortened class periods, this is how we start class. No matter what is on the agenda or how much we have to cover, whether I'm teaching middle school students or seniors in college, every day begins with students getting the opportunity to identify and share something positive happening in their lives.

It's a routine; students know that this is how the period starts in Mr. Muir's class, and whether work is hard or not that day, whether the lesson is exciting or boring, whether they're having a good day or a bad one, there will always be three minutes dedicated to positivity.

From the outside-looking-in, starting class with "Good Things" may seem to just be something we do for fun. Some might even consider it frivolous as it is not connected to learning targets or class content. "In a 55-minute class, how can you dedicate 3 of them to talking about Fortnight and soccer games?!"

However, the reason I've always started class this way is not just to have fun, and if I'm being honest, it's not because I'm that curious about every single event in my students' lives. The truth is, I don't really care if you beat Fortnite. It's because this routine reinforces positive affirmations at the start of every class. Research conducted by UW Medicine shows that regular positive affirmations can have a measurable effect on a person's "well-being, stress level, and academic performance."[1]

This is where the shift in mindset has to happen. Like building relationships, having fun routines that are disconnected from content standards or curriculum is not frivolous, but essential, if they serve the purpose of binding a class together.

"Good Things" is a calculated way for students to get the most out of every class period. Like many teaching approaches, while not always obvious, there is a method to the madness. It's a routine to help establish classroom culture, a shared set of values that unify the group and create a sense of cohesion. These collective values form the foundation for all of the learning that happens in the classroom.

Defining Collective Values

Often, these values go unnoticed. They function like white noise buzzing in the background. Sociologists, anthropologists, and philosophers differ in how to define values but they generally cover what a group considers fair, just, important, and good. Often, values conflict as in the case of valuing safety and freedom or individual accomplishments and collective responsibilities.

Shared values exist in tight-knit smaller communities, and within entire nations and cultures. They exist within the classroom as well. As educators, we can help students make these values visible by creating a set of shared values. A classroom is still one of the remaining locations where a population remains truly diverse. In an era of echo chambers and filter bubbles, the classroom is a place where students will be exposed to a broader range of ideologies and worldviews.

Each community will have a beautiful mosaic of diversity, ranging from socio-economic backgrounds to cultural identity to family structures to religious affiliation to ideological backgrounds to linguistic experiences. We have the opportunity to embrace the diversity of each student's lived experience. However, we also want the classroom community to identify shared values that they have in common in order to build bridges with each other.

Here is an example of how you might help students identify commonalities and shared values.

Part 1: Start with a Personal Reflection   Begin by having students engage in personal reflection. By first reflecting on themselves, they will be better suited to connect with others. Here are some potential reflection questions:

- What do you care about the most in life?
- Think of the kind of person you want to be. What are some things you can do to be that person?

- What are four qualities you value in a friend?
- What is a life rule that you wish everyone followed?

In an early elementary classroom, you might start by reading a picture book together to set the tone. Or you might ask them to draw a picture of the kind of person they want to be rather than writing it out as a warm-up. At an older age, you might go more advanced with a question like, "What are some values in our society that you agree with? What are some you disagree with?"

Part 2: Discuss with a Partner In this phase, you might use a set of sentence frames to guide the conversation. Or you might keep it open-ended and see how students do. You might expand it with a question like, "How were your partner's ideas similar or different from yours?"

Part 3: Silent Writing Have a set of questions or prompts written on the whiteboard or on chart paper throughout the classroom. A few options might be:

- In our class, we value. . . .
- We should all agree to. . . .
- Explain our classroom's community values using only symbols or pictures.
- What kind of a classroom space do you want to share?

Students then answer these questions and prompts silently. There's something powerful about the shared silence as students share their ideas publicly and engage in ongoing conversations without ever speaking a word. Often, some of the shy students will "speak up" in these moments with bold words and symbols.

You can run this process as a carousel activity or allow students to move freely from location to location. It can help to partner students with one person being a reader and the other a writer, and then ask them to switch back and forth.

Part 4: Debrief Have students debrief the activity with reflection questions:

- What was this like for you?
- How did you feel?

- What are some areas where our class might disagree?
- What are some shared trends that you notice?

For older students, you might expand this activity into a larger Socratic Seminar, where students take the initial reflection questions and engage in a deeper discussion on the topic.

Part 5: Identify Values   Together as a class, create your set of shared values. In some cases, you might ask students to vote on the values and see if there is a true sense of consensus. You might rewrite certain values. But in the end, the group should have a set of core values that the whole group can agree on.

Part 6: Turn These into Actions   This is where students help create norms and expectations to help ensure their collective values are upheld. One way to do this is the Class Contract.

The Class Contract

Following exploration of shared values, students help design a contract that clearly states what the expectations for behavior and norms are early in the school year, but is also an accountability tool throughout. It is an agreed-on document to reference proactively or when violations of the contract occur.

To create a class contract with students, start by having them to think about what a healthy class is. Perhaps ask:

- What does a healthy class *look* like?
- What does a healthy class *sound* like?
- What does a healthy class *feel* like?
- What kind of class do you learn best in?

If they are able, have students write their responses to these prompts first, then lead a whole-group discussion where you record all of their responses. If there are certain expectations you want on the contract, steer the discussion at some point to make sure they are covered.

For instance, if disposing trash and keeping your classroom clean is an important value to you, and it is not brought up organically by students, ask the question, "Does anyone just work better when your space just looks nice?" Several hands will go up. "Yeah, me too. What can we put on the contract that will help the room stay nice and clean?"

Even though you're inserting your expectations into the discussion, it's still being phrased as a question or suggestion. The power of a class contract is that it is student-generated, and those expectations are owned by the students. Therefore, it's as much their responsibility as it is yours to uphold the contract.

Once finished with the discussion, as a class, summarize your notes with clear and concise bullet points. This can go on a physical poster or typed in a document to print out.

Some items to consider including on your class contract:

- Respect for peers
- Respect for teacher
- Respect for self
- Respect for the learning environment
- Classroom safety
- Inclusion
- Agency and personal responsibility
- Collaboration

Class Contract Gallery Walk

Another activity to create a class contract would be to write each of the preceding headings on a different piece of chart paper, and have students do a gallery walk where they write on the chart paper what those items look, sound, and feel like. If a student sees someone has already written what they were going to contribute, they can put a checkmark next to it. This affirms that that item should be included in the contract. When the gallery walk is complete, as a class, review what everyone wrote, discuss, and create the contract with it.

When the contract is complete, have every student sign the bottom of the poster, agreeing to the terms of the contract. Not only does this form clear norms for the class, you can also now reference back to the contract on a regular basis. Go over it every time you start a new learning unit or project. Have students read it aloud periodically throughout the year. Or when one of the expectations on the contract is violated, which will of course happen—a student is disrespectful, or the physical classroom space is not being taken care of—you have something to reference back to.

You can talk to the class using the contract or pull an individual student aside and say, "Hey, remember that contract we made at the beginning of the year? Do you feel like you're holding up your end to it?" That way there's no surprises when you show your displeasure with unacceptable behavior.

Like everything else, the class contract is a tool and not a solution. It does not magically bind students to your expectations for them and ensure perfect behavior. However, when created with the power of student voice-and-choice and then exercised with intention, it can be used to establish norms for a healthy classroom.

Shared Goals

I (John) sat with my fellow team members planning the service learning aspects of the IMPACT program at our school. Students would brainstorm, plan, and reflect on the projects in this program; however, we teachers would design the overall structure for the program.

At one point, our math teacher clapped his hands and said, "I got it! What we need is a celebration when we hit 1,000 hours of service. That will build momentum for the rest of the school year."

"So, what, like a pizza party?" I asked.

"Yeah, pizza. Banners. Some prizes. Make it big," he said. "We can invite parents and guardians. Celebrate our service learning like you celebrate winning a basketball game," he said.

I shook my head skeptically. "I just . . . I just . . . It feels, um, it feels like that takes the motivation away. You should serve out of the goodness of your heart. That's the motivation. If we make it about a prize, what's the point? I'm not even sure we should keep track of the number of service hours."

"Yeah, I hear you, but we all do this in life. We value what we track. If you value money, you're constantly checking stocks and bank accounts. You value fitness? Chances are you're tracking the miles you run or the weight you lift. Communities do this, too. We value what we track. Then, when we hit goals, we have celebrations."

"Yeah, but this isn't money and it's not a football game. It's social. It's not competitive," I point out.

"Okay, okay, but hear me out. You're married, right?"

"Yeah."

"Do you plan to celebrate your 10-year anniversary in a few years?"

I nod.

"But that's not your motive, right? Your motive is that you love your wife. But you still track the number of years you've been married. You pay attention to your anniversary each year. Even at this level, you track your data. Even in the smallest of communities, the nuclear families, we do this. Your kid has a birthday. Congrats on staying alive for one more circle around the sum."

I was skeptical at first, but he was making a great point. I eventually agreed that we should track the number of service hours. We put up a poster with a thermometer and shaded it in for each service hour recorded. There were certainly a few students who volunteered simply to move up the numbers, often as a result of positive peer pressure. But to my surprise, these students began to develop empathy with the community. They started serving from an intrinsic desire to help others. And the celebration? Well, it was everything we wanted and more. We had pizza and banners and balloons and even karaoke.

Later, we expanded the data tracking to include individual students and a leader board. This backfired. Certain students grew fixated on being the leaders and they lost focus on the goal of empathy and kindness. Others gave up entirely. Instead of working toward a shared goal, they viewed themselves as competitors.

This experience was a reminder of the power of goal-setting and celebrations as a shared classroom community.

Consider the following:

- **What are your main focus areas for your goals?** Do you want to track student achievement on tests? Do you want to measure overall assignment completion rates? Do you want to focus on something like student behaviors?

- **What types of goals do you want to craft?** You might focus on certain key achievements like hours served in service learning or achievement levels on tests (what percentage of students passed the district benchmark). Other goals might focus on growth instead. So, a reading fluency goal might be the number of students who improve by one reading level. Still other goals focus on habits. These often include keeping track of a streak. It could be something as simple as the number of days in a row that students are on time for math centers.

  Some nuance here. The wrong kinds of goals can backfire. Avoid creating goals where students are competing against each other. This gets in the way of the shared goal-setting process. The more collaborative the goal, the more shared buy-in from students to achieve it.

- **How will you track the progress?** The entire class should see not only the data, but also their progression toward the goal. You might use a progress bar, a thermometer, a set of circles students color in, or a checklist with boxes to cross off. At a younger age, you might have a paper chain with small loops of construction paper that students tear each time they progress. Or it might be a marble jar. In these moments, the goal tracking is not only visible, but also a sort ritual that students share together.

- **How will you celebrate?** Consider the reward or celebration you will have when the whole class meets a shared goal. You can bring students into this discussion as well. Extended silent reading time? Play board games? Wear pajamas to school?

The First Week of School

Building culture starts on day one of the school year. The first week of school is your student's first impression of your class (and you know what they say about first impressions). It is within those first few days of the school year that students form those initial impressions of your classroom that they will carry the rest of the year. Of course, that impression can change as the year progresses, but what you and your class deem important in week one will establish that importance throughout the year.

I (Trevor) often give the advice to avoid too much content work during the first week of the school year. Let the first week be about culture-building, setting norms and expectations, and then dive into content in week two. I share that this investment will pay dividends the rest of the year. Often when I share this idea on social media, I'm met with responses from teachers like, "I wish I could do that, but I have way too many content standards. I have to get started right away" Or, "My students need to get into the routine of my class, and that routine includes schoolwork."

I get that. Dedicating a week to building culture can seem like a big investment, especially when you really do have a lot of content to cover and little time to cover it. However, and this can't be stated strongly enough, intentional culture-building is a worthwhile investment. The first week of school is where you set the tone for your class, introducing expectations for the learning environment your students will engage in for the rest of the school year. It's where you meet students and they meet you. You are introduced to their learning styles, and they first witness your teaching style.

This isn't to say that you need to be perfect the first week of school, or even that you have to make every student love your class in week one. There's no such thing as a perfect teacher and making students love your class should not be your top objective (more on that later). Instead, it's a call to be deliberate about culture-building in week one because how students feel about your class after the first week is often indicative of how they'll feel about it the rest of the year.

In fact, in a study conducted by Loyola University Chicago, students were asked to rate their professors following their first class with them.[2] Then they reassessed the professors' performance at both the midpoint and the conclusion of the semester. Interestingly, the ratings professors initially received closely mirrored the ratings they received after the course concluded. Even after an entire semester with that professor, students exhibited little variation in their opinions about them, demonstrating the power of the first impression.

Planning the First Week

As you are planning the first week of school, ask the question, "How do I want my students to feel and what do I want them to know about my class?" You cannot puppeteer your students into feeling a certain way, and you can't force them to know everything you want them to know. This is a lesson that will carry on far beyond the first week. However, you can plan activities that help pave that strong foundation at the beginning of the year.

What are the key tenets of the culture you want in your classroom?

- Freedom of expression?
- Eager learners?
- Student empowerment?
- Collaborative environment?
- Hard-working learners?
- Respectful learners?

Take some time to consider this question, and then spend some time planning activities that introduce these themes in week one of the school year. Again, these themes need to be reinforced throughout the year, but their introduction to students matters.

For a full week of free lesson plans to build a positive class culture in week one, access the Digital Download First Week at newteachermindset.com.

Notes

1. Boynton, Emily. (2021). How to practice positive affirmations—and why they work. Right as Rain by UW Medicine. https://rightasrain.uwmedicine.org/mind/well-being/positive-affirmations
2. Loyola University Health System. (2010). The importance of making a good first impression in the classroom. https://phys.org/news/2010-12-importance-good-classroom.html

CHAPTER
5

Classroom Rituals for Self-Directed Students

Life is full of little rituals. At our (John's) home, we don't have assigned seats. However, each of my kids has a seat they have claimed at the island (the countertop in our kitchen—not the geographical feature—unfortunately, we don't own an island). When I play catch with my sons, there is a ritual of putting on a glove that reminds me of some of my fondest childhood memories playing catch with my dad. When I draw pictures with my daughter, there is a ritual of taking out the art supplies and anticipating what we will create.

In both the mundane and the profound, we find rituals. Weddings, funerals, breakfast, starting a car—these all require ritualistic knowledge. When you check out at the grocery store, you follow a ritual, from the guesswork moment of "which line is faster?" to the moment you receive your receipt. When you empty the dishwasher, take out the trash, or sweep the floor, you follow a ritual as well. These rituals form the rhythm of our lives. The fact that they are automatic doesn't make them any less powerful.

A ritual isn't necessarily a rule so much as an unspoken process that dictates how we live. The best rituals are natural, informal, flexible, and motivated by love. For this reason, we prefer to view class procedures as rituals to be practiced rather than procedures to be followed. Rituals grow stronger the longer we do them—and grow most powerful when they become automatic.

Students walk in on the first day unsure of how things work. If they're older, they'll probably have a general sense of where to go and what to do. But the classroom space is unfamiliar and the expectations are unclear. Over time, if the rituals are unclear, the classroom can devolve into chaos. Students can feel unsure or even anxious about the expectations. In these moments, teachers might even discipline a student for a specific action that doesn't actually violate any class rules so much as a failure to understand the rituals.

As a new teacher, I (John) viewed rules and procedures as rigid systems that I created for my students. My job was to teach those to my students so they could follow the system. Slowly, I shifted my mindset from "How do I get students to follow the system?" to "How do I adapt the system to fit the students?" This new mindset focused on empowering students to co-design the class rituals with a focus on purpose and intentionality.

Here are some of the fundamental characteristics of rituals to adopt in your classroom.

Great Routines Should Be Purposeful

In my (Trevor) first year of teaching, I was paired with a co-teacher whose middle name may have been "Routine." She was as type-A as any person I'd ever met, desiring structure and order within every aspect of her life and our classroom. I, on the other hand, have never had a strong penchant for structure. Each day is a new day, so why order your days as if you can expect what is to come? I never kept a calendar, regularly planned lessons the night before, or allowed spontaneity to direct my life and work.

As a chronic procrastinator growing up, this posture always seemed to work for me. Maybe it explained my less-than-stellar GPA in school, but I seemed to be doing just fine living without too many routines. Creating structure and routines requires discipline and hard work, so if I could get by without them, why dedicate the effort?

But I soon found that my lack of structure drove my co-teacher crazy. One day she sat me down and told me that I needed to start being more organized.

"Sure, I'll try." I responded.

"No, you can't try. You *need* to. Or I just won't be able to teach with you anymore."

At first I thought she was being a little extreme, but as the school year progressed, my lack of structure started to drive me crazy as well. My lessons were inconsistent, class took too long to begin, student work piled up on my desk (making grading a nightmare), and I could see that the chaos was overwhelming some of my students and *especially* my co-teacher. Nobody thrives when they are overwhelmed.

Articulating the Purpose of Routines

I quickly identified a good reason for developing solid routines in my classroom because I was discovering the lack of discipline and effort was actually leading to a far greater expenditure of effort for everyone, myself included. Like many aspects of education and life, purpose was a strong motivator to activate the evolution of my practice.

The same applies for students. If we can articulate the purpose of a routine and help students understand its value, we can help reduce their stress and anxiety by providing a sense of structure and predictability in our classrooms. This can be especially helpful for students who are prone to feeling overwhelmed by uncertainty or change.

When developing routines or evaluating the ones you already have, try to explain the rationale for each one. If there is an expectation for students to submit an exit ticket at the conclusion of every class period, ask what the objective is for that. Is it a formative assessment to gain insight on your students' understanding? Are exit tickets an opportunity for them to reflect and process their learning one more time before leaving? Is it to challenge them with something new that will be covered the next day? Something else? If you ask students to get in a line before going to recess, ask them why a line would be important. If you keep a rotation of a new line leader each day, ask students why they rotate the line leader on the way to specials.

Whatever the purpose is, identify it. Write it out. And then share it with students. Bring them into a conversation. If a routine seems arbitrary, it can create resentment. But when students understand the reason for a routine, they will be much more apt to adopt it, making the class less chaotic, you more stress-free, and your co-teacher less inclined to drive you somewhere out into the country and abandon you there.

Great Routines Should Be Decided Collaboratively with Students

Traditionally, teachers will take the whole first week to go over classroom procedures with the students. Sometimes that's necessary. A science lab might need some tight safety protocols. A kindergarten teacher might need to take some time to explain the basics of how school works. However, there's also value in asking students to help develop the rituals for the classroom community. Here, you work as the facilitator guiding students through the process of creating and negotiating the procedures for your community. The following are some of the benefits of this approach:

- **You start from a place of empathy.** Ask the question "How do I create systems to fit the needs of my students?" rather than "How do I get my students to follow the systems I've created?"

- **Your students experience a sense of agency.** When they get to develop the classroom procedures, they experience more voice and choice in the structures and systems of the community space. This sends a powerful message that they belong and that you value their input.

- **You model conflict resolution early.** This process will include some conflict and you will have some moments of give-and-take. But that's okay. You are modeling constructive criticism and conflict resolution early on in the year.

- **You set the tone for a shared classroom space where every voice is honored.** Students should leave the experience feeling like they have a place in your classroom. Often, when we have a top-down approach with classroom procedures, we send the message that we value compliance more than anything else. But when we ask students to negotiate the procedures, they learn that we value self-direction and collaboration as well.

Routines Should Be Intuitive

I (John) recently visited a restaurant and noticed something throughout the evening. Every time someone walked through the door, they stopped and looked around. Sometimes they searched for a sign. Other times they looked for a person. But each time, they remained unsure about where they were supposed to go. A few potential customers walked back out the door. Others sheepishly headed over to a table, waiting to see if they were following the right procedures. Why the confusion? This restaurant lacked a simple sign that we all expect from a sit-down restaurant.

Most restaurants have one of two signs, either "Please wait to be seated" or "Please seat yourself." Notice the clarity of the signs. There's a simple present tense action verb. It's also polite. Both signs use "please." Finally, both signs contain positive phrasing. It doesn't read, "Don't sit down" but rather "Please wait to be seated." We register the message and intuitively make our next moves.

Intuitive rituals reduce cognitive load so that students can spend less time trying to figure out what to do and more time focused on the learning tasks at hand.

This might not seem like a big deal but if it saves 2-3 minutes per hour, you save 3,240 minutes in a year, which converts to nearly two additional weeks in a school year. Meanwhile, an intuitive design helps students feel relaxed and at ease, which can lead to more optimal learning as well. As a teacher, I have had to shift my mindset from "how do I show students the routines" to "how do I make this so obvious they won't get confused?"

We can have intuitive visuals and statements so that students can practice the routine without needing to learn something new.

- **Where they are supposed to go when they walk in:** An intuitive option might be the word *warm-up* or *bell ringer* followed by clear directions.

- **What they will be doing for the day:** An intuitive option would be an agenda posted on the board in the same spot each day. In an early elementary class, you might keep this color coded with visuals alerting students to the activities.

- **How much time they have for assignments:** An intuitive option would be a visual timer that they can read.

- **Where and when they turn in work:** An intuitive option might be a turn-in bin symbol with a phrase such as "Please turn your work in here" near the exit.

- **The process for leaving to use the restroom:** An intuitive option would be a clearly marked area with a phrase like "sign out" and a small stack of passes students can use where they only need to mark the time and their names along with a binder with the sign-in and sign-out options.

Try This: The Classroom Rituals Grid

On the first day of class, lead your class on a discussion about rituals. Where do they notice rituals in life? Perhaps it's at a church, temple, mosque, or synagogue. Maybe it's on the ballfield or at the theater. Without realizing it, students adopt certain practices. They raise their hands, for example. This is a chance to debrief the current rituals that the class has already silently adopted.

At this point, you can introduce the ritual for getting everyone's attention. You might raise your hand silently and everyone else will do the same thing. Next, you can invite students to help determine the rituals as a class. The goal here is to empower students to own the routines as a classroom community. When they negotiate the rituals as a class, there is an increased buy-in. It doesn't feel arbitrary. In addition, the negotiation process allows students to see the rationale behind our classroom procedures.

The Classroom Rituals Grid process also sends a clear message to students that "voice and choice" go beyond assignments and into the classroom community itself. This strategy empowers students by bringing them into the conversation about procedures in the first week of school. Here's the gist of how it works:

Step 1: Students start with a sticky note where they write down any question they have about what they are allowed to do or not allowed to do in class. They might also ask questions about where items are located, how things are turned in, etc. These are typically questions like, "Am I allowed to use the restroom? Can I sharpen my pencil? Can I throw something away? Am I allowed to get materials?"

Step 2: As a whole class, go through the sticky notes and look at questions that are similar. You can do this by having students read the questions together in a crowd or you can do this by asking the questions as the teacher.

Step 3: Take the most common questions and put them into this rituals grid, which is based on the methods of grouping (individual, partners, small group, and whole class).

Step 4: As a whole class, we collectively decide on the rituals. It helps to encourage students to come up with a strong rationale for their ritual. For example, students might say that headphones are fine individually but they are disrespectful when working with a partner or listening to a teacher.

Step 5: Create an anchor chart or poster with the rituals grid. It also helps to type up the rituals grid up and keep it as a handout for new students who arrive later in the year. Here is a sample rituals grid:

Sample Classroom Rituals Grid.

Question	Individual	Partner	Group	Whole Class
Whom can I talk to?	If you raise your hand, you can talk to the teacher. You may also ask questions of one another. Just keep the volume at a lower level.	You may talk to your partner only, and then if you have a question, go to the teacher. It's important for partners to problem-solve together.	You may talk to your group only, and then if you have a question, go to the teacher. It's important for groups to cooperate.	If you raise your hand, you may participate in any whole-class discussion. Otherwise, people can't hear one another.
Can I throw waste in the trash?	Yes, one at a time.	Yes, one at a time.	Yes, one at a time.	No, it's a distraction to the class.
Can I sharpen my pencil?	Yes, one at a time.	Yes, one at a time.	Yes, one at a time.	No, it's a distraction to the class.
Can I turn in work?	Yes, one at a time.	No, you need to stick with your partner.	Yes, one at a time.	No, it's a distraction to the class.

The Classroom Rituals Grid is a visual representation of how class works. The goal is to increase student ownership and buy-in, while also setting the tone for a class with clear expectations and an intuitive system.

We Need to Practice Routines

The Classroom Rituals Grid is just the starting place. Once you've determined class rituals, you'll still need to practice these. The following are some ideas you might use:

- **Class book of routines:** Students write a picture book demonstrating how the routines work.
- **Act out routines:** Students act out the routines and give peer feedback.
- **Illustrate and guessing game:** Students do an illustration and guessing game in the style of Pictionary.
- **Two truths and a lie:** Students play a game where they have to guess what routines are true and what are lies.

Access these activities at newteachermindset.com.

What to Do When There's a Sub

One of the signs of a truly empowered classroom community is when the students continue to follow the class rituals even when you are absent. However, this takes some intentional foresight on the part of the teacher. If your classroom truly is different from day one, there might be a mismatch between the classroom climate you cultivate and a more traditional substitute teacher. Let's explore what it looks like to prepare for a substitute teacher.

Prepare Your Students in Advance

Somewhere within the first two weeks of school, take 10 minutes out of your class time and talk to your students about how to behave with a substitute teacher. Emphasize the importance of respect, the difficulty of being a sub, and the need to follow class rituals. If you know in advance that you will be out, do the initial instruction and share your expectations for the next day (so that students are genuinely prepared).

You may need to go over the following information:

- What students can and cannot do
- How to handle issues like attendance
- The importance of the class volunteers in helping the class run smoothly
- The fact that you trust your class and you realize how ridiculous this seems
- You will have little tolerance for misbehavior around the sub

You might also need to remind students that substitute teachers may have a different set of expectations regarding noise, movement, and so on. Talk through this with your classroom and ask them to be respectful of the guest teacher. It can help to have specific classroom jobs that students do with corresponding roles and responsibilities.

From there, you can prepare for the substitute teacher in advance by sharing a description of how your classroom works. In a truly empowered classroom, the students should be able to run many aspects of the classroom systems on their own. But they should also be adaptable enough to handle a substitute teacher who might not be as comfortable with this level of student self-direction. The key is that you talk through this potential challenge together with your class so they can anticipate it.

Access the free Subfolder Template at newteachermindset.com.

Navigating Boundaries: Balancing Rules, Boundaries, and Flexibility

One time I (Trevor) had this idea to have my students go outside and have a contest to see who could build a campfire using just three matches and a pile of sticks, and it would all be in the snow in the dead of winter. But first, we would read the short story *To Build a Fire* to get some ideas and inspiration. I mean, talk about connecting literacy with something fun.

So we read the story and hiked out of my classroom into the woods by our school and we built a fire. And it was epic. But then when we got back in the school, my students smelled like campfire, and my principal received a complaint. So he said, "Are you planning on doing this with the rest of your classes today?" I said, "yes," I was. And he said, "Yeah, I don't think you're going to be able to. Building fires outside the school and the smoke smell might not be the best idea."

And so I said, "Yeah, I understand." But after he left, I was pretty bummed about this. I was really excited about connecting this piece of literature with a fun, hands-on learning experience, and I saw in that first hour class how much students loved it. So when my next class came in, I wasn't excited about breaking the news to them that we couldn't go outside.

But just as I was starting to make that announcement, my principal popped his head back into my classroom and said, "Never mind, Mr. Muir, go out and build the fire."

He changed his mind.

And so we spent the day reading and building campfires. And we roasted marshmallows too. After school, I asked my principal why he changed his mind, and he said it was because he overheard students from my first hour talking about how much fun they had, and he figured it was worth getting a few complaints to see high school seniors that were excited about English class.

What I love about this, what I love about his leadership here, was that it was adaptable. His decisions weren't fixed, but instead flexible to the situation. He allowed them to be informed by further information. This was such a valuable lesson for me as a teacher. So many times I've held rigid rules and felt conflicted when there seemed to be a good reason to push those boundaries, but I thought I couldn't because they were already stated.

Like when you're teaching writing and saying your poems have to rhyme, but then a student turns in something brilliant that doesn't rhyme and you mark them down for it. Or you're saying students need to solve this math problem this way, but they do it another way and still get to the right answer, and you say "that's wrong." Or you're saying that during reading time, students need to be silent, but then two kids geek out about a book they're reading together, and you tell them "no talking."

Firm boundaries are important (as stated throughout this entire chapter), and I understand the need for rhyming in poetry, learning math in a certain way, or the benefits of a quiet room for reading. I do.

But sometimes it's okay to move outside of those boundaries. In terms of rituals, there's a time to break away from the routine and do something entirely different. We need routine, but we also need novelty.

It's easy to get stuck doing things a certain way because that's always how it's been done. And yet sometimes we learn that there are other paths to take. There's good reasons to change our minds, be flexible, maybe even break our own rules.

Within reason, of course. If my principal assessed that building fires were dangerous or disruptive to other classes, of course, he should stay firm on his decision and rule. But when he weighed the outcome and saw that a little flexibility was worth it, students got to experience a little extra joy in English class, I got to feel trusted and honored by my school leader, and I also got to eat a bunch of marshmallows at work that day.

Class Routines Checklist

Here is a checklist to help you establish essential routines in your classroom.

- Morning Routine:
  - Greeting students as they enter the classroom.
  - Setting up a morning task or activity for early arrivals.
  - Establishing a routine for attendance.
- Organizational Routines:
  - Designating specific places for backpacks, coats, and personal belongings.
  - Implementing a system for turning in and collecting assignments.

- Establishing a system for distributing and collecting textbooks, notebooks, and other learning materials.
- Implementing a routine for checking and replenishing classroom supplies.
- Transition Routines:
  - Establishing signals or cues for transitions between activities.
  - Providing a countdown or timer for transitions.
- Classroom Management Routines:
  - Developing a system for behavior expectations and consequences.
  - Implementing a reward system for positive behavior.
  - Holding regular class meetings to discuss expectations and address concerns.
- Lesson Start and End Routines:
  - Beginning each lesson with a clear agenda or learning objective.
  - Implementing engaging lesson starters or warm-up activities.
  - Concluding lessons with a summary and preview of upcoming topics.
  - Giving exit tickets for the end of each class.
- Homework and Assignments:
  - Establishing a routine for assigning and collecting homework.
  - Clearly communicating expectations for completing and submitting assignments.
- Communication with Parents:
  - Setting up regular communication channels with parents (newsletters, emails, etc.).
  - Scheduling parent-teacher conferences and providing updates on student progress.
  - Establishing a system for addressing parental concerns or inquiries.
- Technology Integration:
  - Establishing guidelines for the use of technology in the classroom.
  - Ensuring students understand and follow digital citizenship rules.

- Classroom Cleanup Routine:
  - Assigning specific tasks for students to clean up after activities.
  - Establishing a routine for maintaining a tidy classroom.
- Assessment and Feedback:
  - Establishing routines for giving and receiving feedback on assignments.
  - Setting a schedule for quizzes, tests, and other assessments.
  - Providing clear expectations for grading and returning assignments.

Classroom Space: Designing with Empathy and Intentionality

When I (Trevor) was a new teacher, I made it my mission to denounce everything about the traditional classroom space. I learned in college about how the modern classroom was originally designed to prepare students for life working in factories.

Sit in rows because you will someday stand at an assembly line in the same orientation. When the bell rings, you can move to your next class because someday that factory bell will signal the same type of movement. These desks weigh 100 pounds because why would you ever need to move them? They just need to face the front of the room where the teacher stands, which is the center of all learning and instruction.

The overhead fluorescent lights are to imitate the lighting of a factory floor, so you better get used to it in school because you will spend the rest of your life under them at work.

No need to decorate the walls of your classroom with frivolous art. The factory is a place of work and productivity, and the classroom should be as well.

Yet, as a young teacher, I was aware that most of my students would not work in factories like they did at the beginning of the 20th century. And the ones who did most likely would not be in ones that resembled those when the modern education system was designed. The workplace has changed, and yet the primary physical classroom design hasn't.

From a TEDx talk to blog articles to staff meetings, I made it known everywhere I could that the modern classroom is outdated and ineffective. This zeal for protesting the traditional classroom space primarily originated from my own time as a student. Most of my secondary school experience was spent in rows sitting in desks that probably had gum my grandfather stuck under them 50 years prior. I used to always try to find the desk farthest from the teacher so I could attempt to nap without being caught. And when that was not an option, I'd count the holes in the drop ceiling, or read the fading inspirational posters that were hung on the walls before I was even born.

So often these spaces did not inspire me, and I was quick to blame "the system" that I thought desperately needed reformation.

So on top of being highly vocal about the need to abolish the traditional classroom, I decided to model that reform on my own. To start, I made a "no rows" rule in my room. Desks were set up in groups, and while I regularly changed who sat in these groups, the orientation of the room was always in at least pods of four.

To do away with the fluorescent lights, I placed tape over the light switch and put lamps from Goodwill all over the classroom. I wanted my students to feel like they were in a coffee shop rather than a classroom.

I covered the walls with colorful posters and artwork. I even bought an 8' × 15' wallpaper and covered an entire wall with vibrant art. My classroom setting became the place I would want to learn in, and it would serve students in the same way.

The Problem with Abandoning Best Practices

Here's a question for you: Have you ever tried to explain the consequences of the Industrial Revolution for 15 minutes to a group of 14-year-olds?

I hadn't either when I made the "no rows" rule in my classroom. It turns out it's hard to lead direct instruction or deliver complex instructions when half of your students are sitting in groups facing the other direction.

Or have you ever tried to help a student with attention-deficit/hyperactivity disorder (ADHD) focus when they are surrounded by posters and artwork covered in text and images? Me either, and my abundant artwork led to a neurological overload for a number of my students.

How about silent reading in dim lighting where students can't clearly see the words on a page? Antique nightstand lamps seemed like such a great idea.

Like in many other aspects of learning to be a teacher, I soon discovered that not all traditional practices need to be abandoned. Of course, there are aspects of the industrial model of classroom design that need to be updated, which we will get to in a moment, but some are tried-and-true. They've lasted through the ages because they have achieved a certain degree of effectiveness throughout time.

For instance, when giving a lecture, which still belongs in the modern class (we dive deeper into that in the chapter on student engagement), the best orientation is one that is focused on the lecturer. And often the best seating arrangement for this is for desks or tables to be aligned in rows. The audience benefits from having a direct view of the speaker, allowing them to observe body language and hear clearly. The speaker benefits from having a more attentive audience and getting to read their body language, adjusting their delivery accordingly.

When giving direct instruction, rows are not the enemy.

However, during class discussion, rows can be extremely limiting. Your discussion partners are limited to those on your left and right, unless you're along the wall and then you only have one person to discuss with. The same goes for meaningful collaboration and group projects, and they're also not ideal for introverts who need space away from others at times. Rowed seating or other traditional classroom arrangements are still useful when the learning experience calls for it, but only when the learning experience calls for it.

The Case for Flexible Furniture

Think about it like the setting of a story. It would not make much sense if *The Lion King* took place in New York City. That story requires the savannas of Africa and landscapes that allow that story to unfold. The same is true for the classroom. If a learning experience is meant to be hands-on and collaborative, the space must be designed to allow that to happen. Desks can be pushed together for groups to face each other. Perhaps a longer table can be designated for hands-on maker work. A horseshoe of chairs can be set up in a corner for the teacher to pull groups aside to differentiate or deliver mini-lessons.

But if there's direct instruction, rows might be the best option.

This is why the advent of flexible, movable furniture in the classroom can make such a difference. It allows the teacher to adjust the classroom furniture to meet the needs of the learning experience. *The teacher can create a setting to fit the story*. For example, tables and chairs with wheels allow you to be intentional with your space and adapt to the needs of your students.

Form and Function

There is a principle in architecture and design that "form follows function." Essentially, the function of an implement trumps the design of it. The shape of a building or space within it serves the function of that building or space. In the classroom setting, this makes sense. I worked in a school that was experimenting with a company's prototype education furniture. One of the pieces of furniture in the classrooms was a restaurant booth in the corner of the room. The intent was for students to have a comfortable space to sit across from each other.

However, it wasn't long before students figured out that this booth was a great place to hide from the rest of the class. The students sitting at it were hidden from view unless you were standing directly in front of them. It became the space where the gamers went to game, nappers went to nap, and a couple went to kiss (*very awkward having to break that up*). Not to mention, the booth was huge and took up a lot of classroom space, so there was really only room for one in the classroom. This meant it could only serve four students at a time.

Its form was attractive, but its function in this setting was not.

This is the litmus test of whether a piece of furniture or design belongs in the classroom: Does form follow function? Does its form allow it to function in this setting as you want it to?

The Importance of Form

Now, this litmus test does have one kink in it. Renowned architect Frank Lloyd Wright designed the Guggenheim Museum in New York City, which houses some of the 20th century's most important art. The museum looks like nothing else in the city with its spiraling, continuous ramp that takes visitors to a domed skylight with a view of the surrounding skyscrapers. It looks like an elegant white beehive in the middle of the traditional gothic buildings of Manhattan.

Wright received criticism that his design of the museum is unnecessary and frivolous. Museums are for viewing art, they're not supposed to be art themselves. Wright was accused of catering to form over function.

But as the people who become known as "renowned" usually do, Frank Lloyd Wright redefined the concept of form following function. He wrote in a letter explaining his design of the Guggenheim, "Form follows function—that has been misunderstood. Form and function should be one, joined in a spiritual union."[1]

I like that. It's saying functionality is, of course, important, but so is how it looks and feels. The look and feel of a classroom can play a huge role in how students engage and work in it. Here's a few items to consider when designing the form, the look, of your classroom.

Bright and Busy Can Be Distracting   Excessive visual stimulation can overwhelm students and lead to cognitive overload. You've probably seen those classrooms on Instagram and Pinterest that are bursting with color and every square inch of wall space is covered by posters, artwork, and decorations, and of course, those classrooms are beautiful. But they can also be highly distracting, and not only for your neurodivergent students.

According to researchers in psychology at Carnegie Mellon University, a study revealed that children placed in highly decorated classrooms exhibited increased distractions, spent more time off-task, and showed smaller learning improvements compared to when the decorations were absent.[2]

In this study, 24 kindergarten students participated in six introductory science lessons focusing on unfamiliar topics. Three of these lessons took place in a classroom adorned with numerous decorations, while the remaining three lessons occurred in a minimally decorated classroom. The findings demonstrated that although children learned in both classroom settings, they exhibited greater learning gains when the room had fewer decorations.

Blank Walls Can Feel Sterile and Uninspiring   On the flip side, having bland classroom walls can fail to provide any stimulation to students. Colors can have a significant influence on a student's psychology, capable of shaping their moods and emotions. For instance, psychologists have determined that colors such as blue and green evoke feelings of tranquility and composure. On the other hand, shades like red, yellow, and orange can impart warmth and a sense of welcome, but they also have the potential to trigger anger and hostility.

Research has shown that exposing students to the color red before an exam leads to negative outcomes, heightening their frustration and negatively impacting their performance. On the other hand, the presentation of the color blue before a test has been associated with positive effects. Therefore, considering that blue induces calmness and red can evoke excitement or anger, what emotions do you think the color white produces?

Probably not any. So while it's possible to overdesign your classroom and cause overstimulation, it's just as easy to underestimate and have a classroom design that does not help produce the emotions you want your students to have in your class.

Color Scheme Over Content   To help find the median between overstimulation and understimulation, perhaps focus on the color scheme for your classroom rather than the content that will go on your walls. The primary colors of your classroom will likely do more to support a productive, safe, and engaging setting than quotes on posters. As mentioned earlier, colors help dictate mood and behavior, meaning the design of your classroom is directly tied to classroom management.

So either use wall paints (if you are allowed and have the resources for that) or simple artwork with colors that help set the mood in your classroom. What if you have a designated "quiet corner" in your room for independent work, reading time, or the many other reasons you'd want a calming zone for, and in this corner, you hang a world map with calming blue waters and inspiring green land? If you teach elementary and your students regularly sit on a rug during story time or for direct instruction, try a yellow one. Yellow is often associated with happy, energetic, and creative emotions. Take some time to consider the moods and emotions you want your students to have in your classroom, and then choose your color scheme accordingly.

We Work Better When Connected to Nature   Biophilic design is an approach to architecture and interior design that seeks to connect people more closely with nature. It incorporates elements of nature and natural processes into the built environment to enhance well-being, productivity, and overall quality of life. All of us, teachers and students alike, have an innate connection to nature, and research shows it can have a positive impact on mental and physical health.

Similar to the impact of color, the design choices we make as it relates to natural elements can affect student behavior in the classroom. Making biophilic choices for your class setting can actually be quite simple. For instance, whenever possible, allow natural light into your room. Natural light can improve mood and concentration. Or keep a few house plants in your classroom, and if it makes it easier, ask your class for volunteers to help take care of it.

Can you keep an aquarium in your classroom? How about nature photographs on your wall? Can you take your students outside when the weather is nice? These simple actions can make a huge impact on your students' psyche in the classroom.

Student Input Is Crucial One day as a warm-up, I (John) asked my students to color in a map of the classroom. Any space that they considered to be their own personal space would be yellow. Any space that they considered to belong to the teacher was red. Any space that they considered shared space belonging to the whole class would be green.

I had hoped to see mostly green spaces. However, 9 out of 10 students colored the front, side, and back spaces of the classroom as red. The cabinets and supply areas were nearly all colored red as well. In fact, some of the students colored the spaces in between groups as red, meaning only the actual pods of desks were green. Meanwhile, even though I had never used a seating chart, every student colored their own spot yellow.

This was eye-opening for me. For all my talk of student ownership, my students didn't feel that the space belonged to them. They didn't feel the permission to move around or make choices about the room's design. In their minds, it seemed that this was my classroom. It belonged to the teacher and the students were visitors there.

I had never forbidden students from having ownership over the classroom setting, but I had never made it explicit. So, I made a few changes. I created activities that deliberately moved groups toward the whiteboards, where they were then able to make their thinking more visible. I taught from throughout the room during direct instruction. I sat down at various desks when I took attendance during the warm-up.

I asked students how they would like to arrange seating and considered their responses. Instead of hanging up posters and art of my liking, I dedicated wall space to student-work.

Student-Centered Classroom Design

One year, Michaels was having a huge sale on canvases and so I (Trevor) bought a bunch of them and told students they can have one if they want to design a piece of art for our classroom. To my surprise, students claimed all of the canvases in under a minute. Within a week, an entire wall in my classroom was covered with their unique artwork. This gallery wall became a staple of the classroom, a beloved aspect of the room. And it wasn't just because the art was beautiful (some of it was, but some of it . . . wasn't as much). Instead, this aspect of the classroom belonged to students. It was their expression, their choices, and their work on display.

We need to view our classrooms as belonging to our students just as much as they belong to us. With this mindset, we give ownership of our space to our students.

For most of us, when we were growing up, *it's the teacher's class. They're the boss. This is their room.*

Classroom design is usually reserved for the teacher. But like everything else we are talking about in this book, student-centered learning is the goal. And having a student-centered classroom doesn't mean we just consider students as we make choices for them; it often means allowing them to be at the center of those choices. Allowing them to be a part of the conversation. The more ownership students have of the classroom, the more they see the classroom as theirs as much as yours, the more likely they will protect and care for it.

Differentiate Space for Introversion and Extroversion

The other aspect of student-centered classroom design we need to consider is how the different needs of students can dictate our use of space and design.

In her TED Talk on the power of introverts, Susan Cain described a challenge for introverts at school.[3]

So if you picture the typical classroom nowadays: When I was going to school, we sat in rows. We sat in rows of desks like this, and we did most of our work pretty autonomously. But nowadays, your typical classroom has pods of desks—four or five or six or seven kids all facing each other. And kids are working in countless group assignments. Even in subjects like math and creative writing, which you think would depend on solo flights of thought, kids are now expected to act as committee members. And for the kids who prefer to go off by themselves or just to work alone, those kids are seen as outliers often, or worse, as problem cases.

Essentially, space and pedagogy is either made for collaborative work or solitary work, but not both. It's like there are two possible tracks teachers can be on:

1. Work should be collaborative, interactive, and maybe even a little loud.
2. Work should be quiet and solitary.

However, this dichotomous thinking does not reflect the actual world we live in: sometimes life is busy; other times not. But it also does not meet the needs of all students.

What if we designed classroom spaces in a way that honored introverts and extroverts?

An introvert is someone who tends to feel more comfortable, energized, and focused in solitary or low-stimulation environments. They often prefer quiet, reflective spaces to process information and engage in deep thinking. On the other hand, an extrovert thrives in social settings, finding energy, motivation, and enthusiasm through interaction with others. They enjoy group activities; discussions; and vibrant, interactive learning environments that allow for collaboration and sharing of ideas. Recognizing and catering to both preferences can create a balanced and inclusive learning environment that respects the needs and strengths of all students.

It's also important that students understand that introversion isn't the same as being shy. There are loud, social introverts and there are quieter extroverts. The goal here is to build empathy toward group members and to help them see that introverts and extroverts can contribute to the success of creative collaboration.

Space to Be Quiet and Space to Be Loud

The key to designing these spaces lies in differentiation, considering students' needs and trying to accommodate them in your classroom space. If possible, create spaces for introverts to get away from the noise and chaos of a classroom. This might mean allowing a student to take a quick walk to the library to process their thoughts before re-entering the collaborative space. It might also mean allowing the use of headphones so introverts can escape the noise. You can even design introvert enclaves. This could be a garden outside the classroom or a space in the hallway. It might be a half-wall that separates single pods from the larger group.

Likewise, also include collaborative spaces in your classroom. Give students the opportunity to work in groups. Put an old couch in a corner for students to sit on together. Utilize flexible seating so that students who need time to be social can quickly move into groups, while students who need alone time can stay isolated. Obviously, you will experience constraints to your space, and it can be hard to achieve the ideal setting to accommodate all of your students at all times. However, work with what you are given to meet the needs of both your extroverts and introverts.

The Setting of a Story

When we think about our classrooms as the settings of our students' stories, it forces us to consider how we want those stories to unfold. If through their journeys, we want students to learn how to collaborate and work together, then they need classroom seating that allows for that. If we want our introverts to not experience mental overload as they learn and grow, then we have to provide spaces that help prevent that from happening. And if we want the story that takes place in our classrooms to be vibrant and dynamic, perhaps the ceilings and walls should be as well.

This is where we have to shift our mindset around classroom space. Formerly, the classroom has been viewed as *where* learning takes place. But knowing the essential nature of a story's setting, it is equally as important to view classroom space as *how* learning takes place. Space dictates how students learn and engage in your class.

So whether you are designing your first classroom or redesigning your twentieth, start by asking the question, "What story do I want students to tell about my classroom, and how can the setting support that?"

Classroom Space Checklist

Use this checklist as you set up your physical classroom space or evaluate your current one.

- Seating Arrangement:
  - Flexible seating options to accommodate different learning preferences.

- Accessibility for students with mobility challenges.
- Clear pathways for easy movement and accessibility.
- Classroom Layout:
  - Adequate space for whole-group instruction.
  - Designated areas for small group collaboration.
  - Defined spaces for independent work and focused study.
- Lighting:
  - Natural and artificial lighting that supports a comfortable and focused atmosphere.
  - Adjustable window coverings to manage glare and brightness.
  - Well-lit areas for reading and other tasks.
- Visual Displays:
  - Relevant and purposeful displays that enhance learning.
  - Displays reflect diverse cultures, backgrounds, and perspectives.
  - Minimal visual distractions to maintain focus.
- Organization:
  - Clearly labeled storage for classroom supplies and student materials.
  - Efficient organization of teaching materials and resources.
  - Systems in place for distributing and collecting assignments.
- Flexibility and Adaptability:
  - Configurable seating arrangements for different learning activities.
  - Easily adjustable furniture to accommodate various instructional needs.
  - Consideration for students who may require personalized seating.
- Technology Integration:
  - Accessibility to power outlets for electronic devices.
  - Integration of technology tools that support diverse learning styles.
  - Clear guidelines for responsible and purposeful use of technology.
- Safety and Emergency Preparedness:
  - Clearly marked exit routes and emergency procedures.

- First aid kit and emergency contact information readily available.

- Regular checks and maintenance of safety equipment (fire extinguishers, alarms).

- Communication and Feedback:
  - Systems in place for collecting feedback from students on the classroom environment.

  - Open communication channels for addressing concerns or suggestions.

  - Regular reflection and adjustments based on student feedback.

Notes

1. Frank Lloyd Wright to Harry Guggenheim, July 15, 1958. From Frank Lloyd Wright: From Within Outward (EXH.CAT. New York: Solomon R. Guggenheim Foundation, 2009), 268.
2. Association for Psychological Science. (2014). Heavily decorated classrooms disrupt attention and learning in young children. https://www.psychologicalscience.org/news/releases/heavily-decorated-classrooms-disrupt-attention-and-learning-in-young-children.html
3. Cain, S. (2012, July). The power of introverts [Video]. TED. https://www.ted.com/talks/susan_cain_the_power_of_introverts

Organization: Designing Systems to Avoid the Chaos

A few weeks into my (John's) second year of teaching, a student walked up to me after class and said, "I still don't have the essay back that I wrote. Did you grade it yet?"

"Let me see," I said, sifting through the turn-in bin.

After a few minutes of sifting, I couldn't find it. I double-checked the bin again, but still didn't see the essay.

"I'll find it in just a second," I said as the student stood there with her arms folded.

Right then, the phone rang. When I picked it up, our team leader said, "John, you're late to our team meeting."

"Crap. Is it Tuesday?"

"Yep. Falls just after Monday like always. Every Tuesday we have a team meeting during our prep. Just put it into the calendar, John."

"Got it." I abandoned the turn-in bin, filled out a late pass for the student, and headed to the meeting.

The next day, the same student asked if I found the assignment.

"Um, I'll check this afternoon," I told her.

I forgot to check, so she asked again the next day. I added it to my to-do list and searched through the papers. It still wasn't there.

The next day she asked again, and I told her she could search through my stack of graded papers. I knew I had seen it and even graded it. It was a beautiful personal narrative she wrote about her experiences coming to America.

She stopped by at lunch and frantically searched through the stacks of papers. She opened the cabinets. Searched the bookshelves. She moved methodically through the stacks of papers on my desk yet again. Meanwhile, I searched through my backpack and a box of papers under my desk.

Finally, her eyes welled up with tears. "It's lost," she whispered.

"I'm sure we'll find it," I said.

"It's gone forever. I spent forever on it," she said.

"I'm going to do everything I can to find it," I told her.

Tears continued streaming down her face. "This is for my dad. I want to mail it to him. He's in Mexico, but we write to each other every month and my mom mails some of my work to him. I translated it from English back to Spanish for him and he said he practices learning English with my school work."

"I'm so sorry. I will do everything in my power to find that," I told her.

That evening, I stayed until 9:45 p.m. filing papers. I set up a system of hanging file folders. It wasn't perfect but it was a start. And when I finally found her essay, I placed it in a file labeled "VERY IMPORTANT PAPERWORK." I penned an apology letter and paper-clipped it to the essay.

Up until that point, I had viewed teaching as relational and administrative tasks as boring chores that got in the way of the authentic aspects of teaching. However, I had failed to realize how my flippant attitude toward organization had actually harmed my relationship to my students. Moreover, my lack of organization meant we frequently had to start team meetings late. I had viewed my lack of organization as a small character quirk. It was part of being a "creative type." But I now saw it as unprofessional and even harmful. And as for creativity? Well, my lack of organization was actually an opportunity to solve a problem and build a better system. If I was truly going to be creative in my craft, I needed to design a better organizational system. This was a new mindset for me—one that recognized the role of systems in relationships.

By being intentional with organization, we can create a smoother classroom system that actually encourages deeper community and better relationships. These are the invisible structures that facilitate a more enriching classroom community. One of my first areas that I had to tackle was the paper trail.

The Paper Trail

The paper trail is the connection from the moment something is an idea of an assignment all the way to the moment a student gets the assignment back with teacher feedback. It helps to think about the entire thing from start to finish:

1. **Storing ideas:** Where do you plan to store ideas for lessons and assignments? Where will you store graphic organizers, materials, handouts, and so on? If you are teaching in a project-based framework, where will you store the components of projects?

2. **Storing lesson plans:** Where will you store your lesson plans and unit plans? How will you keep them organized? Is there a way that you have digitally linked the lesson plans and the ideas/materials?

3. **Storing subfolders:** Where will you store your updated subfolders so that you have something prepared if you are absent? How do you remind yourself to update the subfolder? Who has access to the folder on a regular basis? We'll be exploring this idea in-depth later in this chapter.

4. **Storing lesson materials/assignments:** Where will you keep the items that need to be photocopied? Where will you keep the items that have already been photocopied? How do you integrate this with the materials or assignments that are digital?

5. **Passing out papers:** What will be your system for making sure each student gets their papers? If you're using a Learning Management System (LMS), what is your system for providing access to students?

6. **Reaching absent students:** What will you do to make sure that students who are absent get the assignments, notes, and so on? What is your process when the student comes back after being absent?

7. **Collecting assignments:** What is your system for collecting assignments from students? How do you collect them efficiently? How will you ensure that students have their names on their papers? If students submit work digitally, how do you keep the process clean and simple? (In other words, how do you avoid overwhelming students by having them submitting work on an LMS, emailing it to you, saving a shared document, and so on?)

8. **Storing unfinished assignments:** Where do students keep the assignments they have not finished? Do they have cubbies? Do they have their own file folders? Or are they supposed to keep an organized binder? Is there a digital location where they can store work? How do you ensure that you also have access to this?

9. **Storing collected assignments:** Once students have turned in an assignment, where do you store it before you have given feedback or graded it? How do you separate out the assignments that have been graded or not graded?

10. **Inputting grades:** What is your system for inputting the grades after you collect the assignment?

11. **Returning graded assignments to students:** What is your process for getting the assignments back to the students after you have graded everything?

12. **Communicating grades:** What is your system so that students know what their grades are? How will you deal with missing work?

This might seem overly complicated. Twelve different areas? However, when you follow this process and create a paper trail, it ensures items don't get lost and students receive timely feedback.

The Other Paperwork

While the paper trail captures the bulk of the paperwork, there are other key areas you might need to consider.

- **Permission slips:** What is your system for keep track of permission slips, money, and so on?

- **Student data:** You'll likely need to keep track of student data from things like fluency tests, benchmarks, and so on. How will you manage that?

- **District and school communication:** What is your system for keeping up on your communication?

- **Documentation of discipline issues:** How will you document discipline issues? (I personally found that Google Forms worked well because they were time-stamped and then they could be turned into a spreadsheet.)

- **Class newsletters:** How will you organize things like class newsletters that need to go home?

- **Other important paperwork:** How will you stay on top of certification paperwork, clock hours for professional development, and other paperwork that will be critical to professional documentation, certification, and other key areas?

For the other paperwork, develop a system that works best for you. Whether you keep it in physical folders or digital ones, have a place specifically designated for the inevitable paperwork that comes with being a teacher.

Set Up a Master Calendar

Keep one master calendar with all information on it. If you get a handout with a calendar (sports calendars, extracurricular calendars), add the dates to the single master calendar. The following are a few things that you might include:

- Holidays—even the obscure ones. Hooray for Bastille Day!
- Nonholiday "High Energy Days" (think the day after Halloween) that you might want to pay attention to so that you aren't blindsided.
- Staff meetings, team meetings, IEP meetings.
- Professional development days and half-days.
- Days off/vacations.
- Parent-teacher conferences.
- Student birthdays (take note of the students who don't celebrate birthdays, too).
- Family Nights, Curriculum Nights, and Dark Knights (if you are in Gotham City).
- Extracurricular activities, including plays, musicals, sports, and clubs.
- Testing schedule.
- Sports and extracurricular activities.
- Teacher evaluation days (see if you can schedule it in advance).

It can help to keep your calendar open when you check your email. That way, you can easily add dates to your calendar. If someone asks to meet with you, either create a calendar invite or ask them to create an invite. The goal should be to keep everything on a calendar, even if it is a weekly occurrence and you assume you'll remember.

A Student-Centered Approach

After you've designed a system (like the paper trail previously mentioned), picture yourself as a student and ask yourself reflective questions from the perspective of a student. When do I receive the assignment? Where do I store it? Do I know where it's being kept? What expectations do I have about when it will be graded? Where do I access my grades or assignment feedback? Where do I go to get my assignment back? Where do I store it afterward?

Be Clear with the Process

I worked with a high school that had a significant challenge with students missing their assignments. Teachers noticed that students would complete their work but fail to turn it in. Coming out of the lockdown era of the pandemic, students seemed to struggle with the newer blended approach to assignments. I asked teachers to identify how students turned in their assignments. Some of them shared a Google Document. Others used a sharing system on Microsoft. Still others submitted via Google Classroom, while others submitted their work on Canvas. They also collected papers physically with a turn-in bin and allowed students to take pictures of certain assignments that they then submitted via student email. Others had students keep binders and folders that teachers would then grade during binder checks.

With so many assignment submission processes, students felt overwhelmed. Teachers had given students multiple options for submitting work, but the process was often unclear. One team decided to do a poll of students to see their perspective. Based on the data, they streamlined their process. Digital work would go through the LMS. Physical work would be submitted via photograph, either through phones or with the use of multiple class scanners. While they still had challenges with incomplete assignments, they saw a 40% increase in assignment completion.

This was a reminder that the organizational process should be clear for students. When we design with clarity, it can reduce cognitive load. This is especially helpful for students with executive function issues. Here are a few ways to improve clarity:

- **Use a common process.** Have one process for digital work and another process for physical work. This creates consistency for students and helps create a ritual that students follow.

- **Use visuals to create clues and reduce cognitive load.** If you're teaching at the K–2 level, this is probably something that you already do. You have icons that represent certain words. You might use illustrations to show how to do something. However, there are developmentally appropriate ways to use clear visual cues.

- **Use bullet points and lists.** This helps to break up key ideas when giving directions. Create shorter paragraphs. Students will likely be reading online, where longer paragraphs can be harder to read. By creating shorter paragraphs, students will have an easier time focusing on information. This can also increase accessibility and even work as an accommodation.

- **Make use of short checklists** that students can use to stay on track.

Introducing New Students to Your Organizational System

We often spend a good portion of the first weeks of school teaching students about the rules, procedures, and systems within our classrooms. However, when a new student arrives a few months later, they are learning all of this information in a short time. This is why it helps to have an onboarding system. Onboarding refers to the process of integrating and orienting new individuals into a community. It involves providing them with the necessary information, resources, training, and support to help them become familiar with their roles, responsibilities, and the overall community environment.

Here, you create an onboarding packet with the rules, routines, and information about how the course works. You might include a get-to-know-you survey that a student fills out. I found that some of the items in the subfolder actually worked really well in the new student onboarding packet. But a packet can feel impersonal. This is why it helps to connect students with a buddy who will function as a mentor for the first week in the class. If you have classroom jobs, you might ask two to three students to be the onboarding buddies and train them to greet new students, answer questions, and help with the onboarding packet.

In the end, all of these organizational systems take time and attention. However, these systems become the structures that help the community grow. When classroom systems run smoothly, the relationships benefit and the community grows closer.

Organization Checklist

The following is a checklist of areas to organize in your classroom.

- Do you have a storage place for forms and permission slips?
- Do you have a method for informing students of work when they're absent?
- Do you have a method for welcoming new students into the classroom?
- Do you have a method for updating contact information?
- Do you have a method for documenting discipline?
- Do you have a place for students to turn in work?
- Do you have a method of organizing the work you have assessed?
- Do you have a method for turning work back to students?
- Do you have a location for materials that you are borrowing? How about materials that you have borrowed and need to return?
- Do you have a "Lost and Found" for students?
- Do you have a calendar where you have recorded school events, student birthdays, unit plans, and other significant events?
- Do you have a place where you have documented communication with parents and students?

8

The Counterintuitive Art of Student Engagement

When I (Trevor) was a first year teacher, my primary goal was to entertain my students. I equated entertainment with *engagement*. This meant constantly telling jokes and trying to be funny. I had intricate handshakes with six different students. I held poetry slams at the local coffee shops for my English classes, taught entire classes with a Scottish accent, played Weezer Spotify on the sound system while students were working (students considered this the golden oldies). I planned dynamic simulations, gamified lessons, huge projects that were almost always loud and hands-on. I spent many late hours planning after school, was constantly on Pinterest trying to find new ways to spice up the bland walls of my classroom. I rarely if ever sat down during the school day, always on my feet trying to engage every single kid at every single moment.

I did everything in my power to NOT let my class be boring. My mindset toward boredom is that it was the enemy. I thought about it like this: if students get bored, they stop liking me, and if they stop liking me, they stop liking my class, and if they stop liking my class, they will lose all inspiration to succeed in life, drop out of school, and end up in a van down by the river.

Okay, maybe that was a little overdramatic, but I did equate boredom with a lack of engagement and learning. And as you can imagine, this fear and belief was extremely taxing. It takes a significant amount of work and energy to make sure 30 students are having fun 100% of the time.

Over time, I discovered that boredom can be a good thing (an idea we explore later in this chapter). It can actually be a product of high student engagement and it can lead to deeper creative thinking. This is where I needed a shift in mindset, realizing that entertainment and engagement are not the same. In fact, engagement does not even require entertainment.

Instead, student engagement is about two critical components: attention and commitment.

What Do We Mean by *Engagement*?

Teacher and author Philip Schlechty defined *student engagement* this way, "Engagement is active. It requires the students to be attentive as well as in attendance; it requires the students to be committed to the task and find some inherent value in what he or she is being asked to do. The engaged student not only does the task assigned but also does the task with enthusiasm and diligence."[1]

Schlechty focused on two core areas of a task. The first is *attention*. This is the idea that a student should be focused on the specific task, without being distracted. The second is *commitment*. This is the idea that a student should find the task intrinsically motivating and challenging and therefore work toward mastering it. In 2002, Schlechty developed a framework for thinking about student engagement based on these two core ideas of attention and commitment (shown in Figure 8.1).

At the bottom of the figure, you have rebellion, which involves diverted attention and no commitment to the task. This is the student who seems to be acting out and causing disruptions. As a result, they fail to learn from the task.

Next, you have retreatism, with no attention and low commitment. Unlike rebellion, the student in retreat is not actively disrupting the learning, but instead seems to be checked out. This student is often distracted and emotionally withdrawn from the task. As a result, this student learns little or nothing from the task.

At the next level, you have ritual compliance (which was originally called passive compliance). This involves both low attention and low commitment. Unlike retreatism, a ritually compliant student isn't completely checked, but instead is

Engagement
High Attention + High Commitment

Strategic Compliance
High Attention + Low Commitment

Ritual Compliance
Low Attention + Low Commitment

Retreatism
No Attention + No Commitment

Rebellion
Diverted Attention + No Commitment

Levels of Student Engagement

based on P. Schlechty and visualization by R. Rios

FIGURE 8.1 Levels of Student Engagement.
Source: Visualization by R. Rios based on work by Phillip Schlechty.

doing the bare minimum to avoid confrontation. This student will learn at a low level from this task and will not retain it over time.

Next is strategic compliance. Often, this looks like engagement because a student might be performing at a high level. Here, the student has high attention on the task but a low commitment. This student is playing the game of school, focused on things like grades, parental approval, rewards, or class rank. But the learning isn't intrinsically rewarding. As a result, this student will often learn at a high level, but fail to retain the learning or transfer it to a new context.

Finally, you have engagement. This requires both high attention and high commitment. Here, a student completely buys in out of a strong intrinsic motivation by tapping into meaning, choice, and challenge. This student will continue focusing even when the task gets more complex and challenging, and often will choose to learn it even when it is ungraded. This student will learn it at a deep level and transfer it to new contexts. This is why it's important that we, as teachers, focus on how to make the subject intrinsically engaging for all students by tapping into curiosity, creativity, and purpose. When this happens, students are more likely to grow into passionate, life-long learners.

Gain Students' Attention

So as we begin to explore how to truly engage students, let's start with getting their attention.

Most teachers have been through this exact scenario: you try to start class with a line like, "Okay, everyone, we're going to get started." And a couple students might glance up at you, indignant that this teacher is bothering them. So a little louder you say, "Everyone! Time to start class." This gets the attention of a few more students, but still the majority of kids keep talking to each other, ignoring the fact that their teacher is in the front of the room with a face that is becoming redder and redder. Finally, you lose your temper, RAISE YOUR VOICE, the room goes quiet, and you are left feeling a little embarrassed, and even more, frustrated that it takes yelling to get your class's attention.

Struggling to start off a class or return from a group activity is a challenge every teacher faces. However, as important as it is to get your students' attention and be as efficient with time as possible, it doesn't have to be difficult. Here are eight ways to get the attention of even the noisiest group of students without raising your voice or losing your cool.

1. Use a Timer   Having structure to the time students spend in your class can help eliminate the chaos of getting everyone's attention. If you have a screen in your room, project a timer for each activity students are working on. That way, they can see how much time is left and when they will need to redirect to the teacher. If you have an Amazon Echo in your room, you can tell Alexa/Echo to set a timer for ___ minutes. This way, there will be no surprises when you have to get your class's attention (and the device can call them back for you).

2. Stand in the Middle of the Room   Use proximity to students to your advantage. If you are standing at the front of the room, you may be close to the students in the front, but are a whole classroom away from kids in the back. When getting their attention, stand in the middle of the room where you are close to every student. If there is a certain group of students who have more trouble redirecting, stand near them when calling the class to attention.

3. Incorporate Awkward Silence   This one can be difficult at first, and it can seem counterintuitive to stand in the middle of the room and say nothing. However, this is possibly the best way to get your class's attention. Here's how you do it: Say one time, "Okay, everyone, I need your attention." Then stand and wait.

It will probably not get instant results the first time, but students will notice you standing there waiting for their attention, and like magic, will give it to you. You'll see students turn and quiet each other and do all of the work for you. I'm not sure if it's out of shame for making their teacher stand quiet for so long or some type of teacher-Jedi-mind-trick, but pretty soon the time you have to stand quietly vanishes. Kids know you will stand until you have their attention, making them feel awkward, and so give attention immediately.

4. Use Call and Response   This is a great culture-building technique that makes getting the class's attention fun and familiar. The teacher has a regular call out to students, and students know how to respond when they hear it. For instance, the teacher could say something like, "What's up? What's up?!" and the class responds, "You know what's up!"

Other call-and-response ideas: Teacher: "Everybody say Ay yo!" Students: "Ay yo!" Teacher: "Holy moly!" Students: "Guacamole!" Teacher: "Alright now stop!" Students: "Collaborate and listen!" You get the idea. It's a fun way to get attention and get everyone on the same page.

5. Have a Countdown Call-Out   Instead of calling for your class's attention out of nowhere, give them a five-second warning. Try saying, "With me in 5. With me in 4. With me in 3. With me in 2. With me in 1." By the time you get to one, students will have had time to wrap up conversations or finish what they were doing and give you their attention.

6. Turn on a Special Light   Have a light in a central place in the room that, when turned on, means you need the class's attention. This could be a lamp, stoplight, lava lamp, disco ball, or any other type of light that gives students a visual cue to turn their attention back to you.

7. Play Animal Sounds   Play mooing cows, chirping birds, or howling monkeys through classroom speakers when you need students' attention. Not only is it funny, but it will be sure to get the attention of your students when you need it. Because, let's be honest, who is going to carry on a conversation with pigs oinking in their ears?!

Pro tip: Let students decide what animal will be played through the speakers each day. It's fun for them, and makes sure the whole class knows what sounds to listen for when it's time to refocus their attention.

8. "Clap If You Can Hear Me"   This is the timeless classic that has worked across generations. It goes like this: Say aloud, "Clap twice if you can hear me." Students who hear you will clap two times. Now say, "Clap three times if you can hear me." More students will join in clapping. For the third time say, "Clap 11 times if you can hear me." By now, there is no chance that there is a student in the room who does not know that you need their attention. Kids get to burn a little physical energy and you now have their attention. Timeless. Magical.

Student focus begins with getting students' attention. Often, this includes an intriguing idea, a mystery, or a sense of novelty. We'll focus on that in this next section on commitment. But in terms of attention, it is far too easy for a new teacher to start giving directions or teaching a new concept without making sure that every student is fully focused.

Minimize Distractions

Once you have students' attention, it's important that they can remain focused by limiting distractions. Sometimes this is outside of our control. We can't control how often the intercom goes off. Similarly, we will all experience that moment when our class is at peak engagement and suddenly the fire drill goes off.

However, we can limit certain environmental distractions. For example, we can clear the classroom of clutter or excessive decorations on the walls. We might need to institute tight rules regarding technology. Some teachers have a location where students check their phones. You can even set up a charger station so that students can charge their phones while they focus on the assignments. Other teachers have incorporated phones into the lessons in a way that requires active participation.

It helps to understand the emotional elements of distraction. Often, when we are the most distracted, it's because of our mental state. We get overwhelmed by too many tasks so we fail to complete any of them well. We might be anxious about an event on the horizon. Or perhaps we hit frustration with a particular project. In other words, being afraid, anxious, or overwhelmed will ultimately kill our ability to stay focused. The same is true of our students. As teachers, we can help students navigate these distractions.

Create Opportunities for Rehearsal and Retrieval of Information

When I tell people that I (John) teach a four-hour class on Tuesday nights, the initial reaction is nearly always, "How do you keep their attention that long?"

Most noneducators I meet imagine a college class in a packed lecture hall with stadium-style seating and a giant screen where the professor lectures in front of pages and pages of slides all packed full of text. If that were the case, four hours would be way too long. Two hours would be too long. Honestly, an hour would be too long on most nights. I then explain that our four-hour classes are highly interactive with multiple ways to make sense out of the information. We also use brain breaks, incorporate movement, and spend time making sense out of the information we're learning.

While there's a time and a place for a well-crafted lecture, we have a tendency to disengage when faced with too much information. This is due to a phenomenon called *cognitive load* (see Figure 8.2). Our brains can only hold so much new information. In the moment, when we are learning something new, we experience the information as sensory memory. Most of this information will be forgotten, but some of this information moves into working memory. Through a process of rehearsal, we process the information and make sense out of it. The information then moves into our long-term memory, where we continue to use it through a retrieval process.

According to cognitive load theory, we can only process a certain amount of information at any given moment. As teachers, we can reduce the cognitive load on

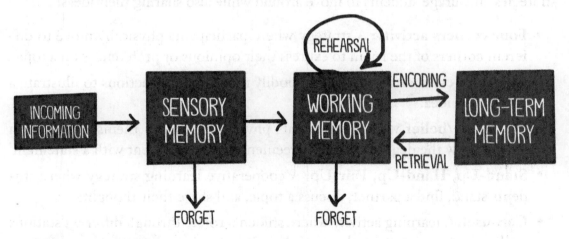

FIGURE 8.2 Cognitive load.

Source: Adapted from Atkinson, R. C., and shiffrin, R. M. (1968) 'Human memory: a proposed system and its control processes.' In Spence, K. W., and Spence J. T. The psychology of learning and motivation, (v.2). New York Academic Press. pp. 89-195" with "Adapted from Atkinson et.al. 1968.

students and allow them to retain more information by creating moments for students to use the information through a rehearsal process. In other words, if you're giving directions for learning a dance move, you can stop at step one and have students practice it briefly before moving to the second move. If you're teaching a big concept like imperialism, you can have students generate ideas of examples or summarize the key ideas relating to imperialism. If you are teaching handwriting technique, pause and let students practice before continuing instruction.

By embedding moments of rehearsal, students can reduce their cognitive load and focus for a longer period of time.

Retrieval occurs when students recall information that they have encoded into their long-term memory. This is what happens when we tap into students' prior knowledge during our lessons.

Even when the information is fascinating, the directions are clear, and the teaching is well crafted, students have a natural tendency to lose attention over time. As teachers, we can be intentional about building in rehearsal and retrieval practice, and information process time.

Retrieval practice should not be entirely verbal. We are far more attentive to a task when we use all of our senses. More specifically, we can aid the retrieval process by using visual, spatial, and kinesthetic elements. Notice how these visible thinking strategies encourage students to move around while also sharing their ideas:

- **Four corners activity:** A strategy where participants physically move to different corners of the room to express their opinions or preferences on a topic.

- **Physical demonstrations:** Using bodily movements or actions to illustrate a concept or idea.

- **Value line/belief walk:** Participants physically position themselves along a line to show the degree of their agreement or disagreement with a statement.

- **Stand-Up, Hand-Up, Pair-Up:** A cooperative learning strategy where students stand, find a partner, discuss a topic, and share their thoughts.

- **Carousel:** A learning activity where students rotate through different stations or discussion points to gather and share information.

- **Graffiti board:** A surface, often a large sheet of paper, where individuals write or draw their thoughts and ideas.

- **Total Physical Response in vocabulary:** A language teaching method that involves physical actions and gestures to help students learn and remember new vocabulary words.

- **Peer feedback gallery walk:** Students review and provide feedback on each other's work displayed around the room.

- **Jigsaw:** A cooperative learning strategy where students become experts in a specific topic and then share their knowledge with a group.

- **Chalk talk:** Silent, written discussions on a large shared surface, like a chalkboard or whiteboard.

- **Fishbowl discussion:** Small groups have a discussion in the center while others observe, then they switch roles.

- **3-2-1 reflection:** Students identify three things they learned, two questions they have, and one thing they found interesting after a lesson.

- **Inside-outside circle:** Students form two concentric circles and discuss a topic, with the inner circle rotating periodically for new interaction.

Pay Attention to the Pacing of Your Lessons

In football, new quarterbacks often make two critical mistakes. The first is that they spend too much time in the pocket reading the field and waiting to find an open wide receiver. These quarterbacks often get sacked. The second kind of quarterback moves too quickly and either runs away from the pocket or throws the ball away, both resulting in a negative outcome.

If you're not a football fan, this might not make sense. But the key idea is that new quarterbacks struggle with the pacing of the game. With multiple players rushing toward them and so much movement all around, it's hard to know what to do. The same is true of improv actors and chefs. In each case, there are so many dynamics and so many skills to move into muscle memory that it's easy to move too quickly or too slowly.

The same thing happens with teachers. Consider all of the things you need to know in a single moment. What am I teaching? How do I make it clear? Do my students understand this? Who is paying attention? Who seems off-task? What strategy do I use next? What is my body language like? How am I communicating? We have lesson plans that help us think intentionally, but we can never quite anticipate the challenge of pacing.

If the pacing is too fast, students grow frustrated and lose attention. They might need an opportunity for retrieval practice or they might simply need some time to make sense out of the new information. In some cases, students (especially English language learners) might struggle to comprehend the language if it's spoken too quickly. On the other hand, when the pacing is too slow, students get bored and antsy. Their body language cries out, "Please move on. Just stop talking about this and go to the next thing!" It's far too easy to over-explain ideas or to give too many examples for the same concepts, and when this happens, we lose our students' attention.

Here are some questions to consider when thinking about pacing:

- Is the pacing developmentally appropriate? Consider how long a first-grade student can sit still. Think about the need of a high school student to have peer interaction.

- Are things moving too fast or too slow? Pay close attention to body language and see if they are anxious (a sign it's moving too fast) or bored (a sign it's moving too slowly).

- Are students getting a chance to move around? Have you implemented brain breaks that incorporate movement?

- Have you broken up the pacing so that students have individual work time and time to work with a partner or a small group?

Show a Progression toward an Outcome

You've probably noticed that students can spend hours playing a single video game without losing much focus. Some of this has to do with the role of novelty and the sheer excitement of the game. Some of this might be social as kids typically play games online with their friends.

However, there's also something else at work. When you play a game, you get a sense of progression from start to finish. It might be a series of levels, a map that you follow, or a timer. Often, you accrue points or gamified coins. But this sense of progression helps users keep their focus and continue gameplay. This sense of progression occurs with novels and TV shows. Whether it's the counter on the screen or the page numbers on the book, you can feel where you are in a story based on visual cues and the overall story arc.

Regardless of the medium, this sense of progression provides immediate cues that answer:

What is the end goal?

Where did I start out and how far have I gone?

Where am I going next?

How far do I still need to go?

We can tap into this same sense of progression in our lesson plans. It starts at the beginning when we tell students where we are heading. This might be an objective, learning target, or driving question that sets the general direction. You might also provide an agenda with a set of activities listed. As you move along, you might have timers for tasks. You might use a progress bar or a set of numbers on slideshows during direct instruction. These small visual cues help students answer, "How far have I gone?" and "How far do I need to go?"

Five Ways to Improve Commitment

My (Trevor's) favorite book of all time is *East of Eden* by John Steinbeck. It was life-changing for me, so much so that I even got an East of Eden tattoo on my arm. If you haven't read the novel, put this book down and go read it. Seriously, go, I'll be here when you get back.

* * *

Something tells me you didn't read all 600 pages since my last paragraph, but that's okay.

Anyway, when I was assigned a senior English class and was deciding what novel I wanted my students to read, *East of Eden* was the first title that came to mind. I thought the theme of the book was perfect for my students, who were just about to embark on the rest of their lives. So we ordered the class text, I assigned it to all of my students, and I told them how much this book meant to me and how much it was going to mean to them by the end of the unit.

I assigned the first chapter and told students that we would be discussing it the next day. So the next day, we all got into a circle to discuss, and about 90% of my students were prepared for discussion. Not exactly what I was hoping for, but not bad odds either. However, after Chapter 2, the number was down to 75%. Chapter 3, 50%. Each day, fewer and fewer students read the book, and more and more turned to SparkNotes to prepare for the activities and discussion. After two weeks of this book, I gave up on it. And now that high school has 120 copies of *East of Eden* collecting dust in a storage closet.

This broke my heart. The next day I had the tattoo removed from my arm.

Okay, not really; it's still there, but I learned a lesson from this experience. Just because I'm excited about a choice I made for my students doesn't mean they will be as well. My enthusiasm was not enough to raise their engagement and commitment levels.

So what can we do to improve the commitment level of students? The following four strategies are my recommendations.

#1: Incorporate Voice and Choice in Your Daily Lessons

If we want students to reach the highest levels of engagement, they need to go beyond full attention and into the realm of full commitment. One way to do this is by providing a sense of autonomy or agency in the learning. This is the sense of buy-in and control that students experience when they have a deeper ownership of the learning process.

When a student has voice and choice, they remain committed to the task at hand. There's a deeper purpose to what they're doing and a sense of control. This can help contribute to a growth mindset, where they persevere when faced with challenges.

Voice and choice might be as small as a set of options or a choice menu. However, it can include every aspect of the learning experience:

- **Choosing the topics:** In reading, this might be a choice of three different articles for jigsaw activity or choice-based silent reading after going to the library. In writing, students might choose whatever topic they want for a Geek-Out Blog. In PE, students might select from several workout stations or team games. In math, they might select which problems they solve from a bank of problems. You might provide students with a choice menu. Regardless of the subject, this is a subtle shift from "How do I make the subject interesting" to "How do I allow students to connect the subject to their interests?" This, in turn, connects to a deeper intrinsic motivation that can help students remain committed to their learning.

- **Choosing the questions:** You might have students engage in a short inquiry-based activity. You might set aside a dedicated time for students to pose questions during direct instruction. You might build in student questions and research into longer projects or let students select which math discourse questions to ask during a lesson. In science, students might develop independent science questions that they will then use for a Science Fair project. In math, it might be a "What Can You Do with This?" problem. Originated by Dan Meyer, students look at a fascinating picture or video and develop their own math question that they then solve.[2] When they tap their curiosity, they are more likely to remain fully committed to the task at hand because they have a deeper drive to find the answer.

- **Choosing the format:** Sometimes students have to learn specific concepts and topics that you teach from a curriculum map. In social studies, for example, students might need to learn about the causes of World War II. However, we can provide a sense of autonomy by allowing students to select the format for what they create or the format for how they learn about the topic (an article, blog post, or video).

- **Choosing the strategies:** This is the idea that students can have a sense of agency not only on what they learn but how they learn it. In math, they might choose which strategy they use to solve a problem. In reading, students might select how they organize their research (a chart, a sketch-note, a spreadsheet, a set of notecards, a binder).

These are just a few ways to empower students with voice and choice. In later chapters, we'll explore student ownership in the assessment process, in selecting scaffolds, and in self-managing the collaborative process in groups. But the core idea is that voice and choice will increase student commitment, and thus, boost student engagement.

Guiding Questions:

1. What are you doing for students that they could be doing for themselves?

2. Look at your standards. Where do you see choice built into them?

3. What are some practical ways to incorporate student ownership into daily practices?

#2: Focus on Relevance

Think about the last time you were fully engaged in a learning task. It might have been a professional development activity with practical insights you could use in your classroom or a podcast you listened to that drew you in through storytelling. Or maybe it was a skill you had always wanted to master and you took the time to learn how to cook or play the guitar or crochet. Whatever it was, you remained committed to the learning because you found it inherently relevant.

There are many ways to define *relevance*. Something might be relevant because it's inherently practical and useful. It might seem relevant because it is deeply personal. It might be more philosophical and connect to big ideas. But it also might simply be novel, fun, or fascinating. Whatever it may be, the driving question is, "Does this matter to me?"

Embedding Relevance   I (Trevor) once gave my students a project where they were asked to tell the entire Romeo and Juliet story in 90 seconds or less. I thought it would be an interesting exercise throughout the reading of the story to have students think about how to summarize the main points of each act, and have a culminating event at the end where they share their summaries. Unfortunately, transcribing old English didn't have the same appeal to high school freshmen as it did to their English-major teacher. After the first act, it was apparent students were not enthusiastic about the ongoing activity. Summarizing for the sake of summarizing was not relevant to these students.

So I went back to the drawing board, searching for a way to add relevance to the task. The next day, I told students that they would be taking their act summaries and creating a script for a YouTube video where they will act out Romeo and Juliet in 90 seconds or less. I said they could choose what their films looked like as long as the audience would understand the story at the end of them.

Students immediately attached to this activity and engaged with the class text. Very little changed about how I taught this unit; students were still reading *Romeo and Juliet* and summarizing the chapters, only now there was a relevant reason for their work. I knew that most of my students use YouTube, Instagram, and TikTok to tell stories and share them. This is a personal motivator for them, and that motivation can carry over to academic engagement.

Identifying Relevance in What You Teach   When I taught social studies, I had students ask, "Why are we even learning this? When will we ever use history?"

My initial temptation to answer this question was to lecture students on the importance of historical literacy to avoid repeating mistakes. Or perhaps to talk about the power of unspoken narratives that shape our worldviews. Or maybe talk about how schools should help students become critical-thinking citizens in a democracy.

Instead, I responded with, "Can you tell me why this isn't seeming relevant to you right now?" This nearly always led to hard personal reflections that ultimately led to lesson redesigns to focus on relevance and authenticity (a topic we'll explore in-depth in a future chapter). It was a hard lesson that it doesn't matter how relevant the content might be if the content doesn't *feel* relevant to the students.

I invited my students to a lunch-time leadership meeting where we talked about how to make social studies connect to our lives. This led to a multimedia project-based learning activity and a service learning activity focused on our local community. But it also led to small changes, like adding more options to the warm-up activity.

Guiding Questions:
- Where is the relevance in what I teach?
- How do I connect what I teach to a real-world content?

- What types of interesting facts will students find intriguing or fascinating?
- How do I connect the learning to deeper stories that will draw students in?
- What practical skills will students be interested in mastering?
- What big ideas connect to deeper, more existential ideas?

#3: Engage in Critical Thinking

Student engagement is more than just active participation. It's what happens when students are fully engaged mentally. This is why critical thinking is so important. Critical thinking includes any kind of analytical thinking that students engage in. It might involve making sense out of a data set in a math class, but also classifying species in a second grade science lesson. It might include comparing and contrasting two characters in a novel, determining the bias of a source, examining the causes and effects of a historical event, testing a hypothesis in science, or organizing information into a concept map.

Students also engage in critical thinking any time they evaluate information. They might rate the impact of various technologies and inventions on the Industrial Revolution, or they might make a claim in a persuasive essay and use facts to support their ideas. It might be a blog post they write, a value line discussion they engage in, or a Socratic Seminar on a big idea. But the key idea is that students should be evaluating information frequently.

In the early elementary level, critical thinking might involve sorting or ranking ideas. It might involve using a math manipulative and having students explain their thinking. It could be a hypothesis about what happens when you mix certain colors together. It could be a Maker Monday activity where students have limited supplies to solve a divergent thinking challenge.

Guiding Questions:

- What are some ways you can incorporate critical-thinking peer discussion questions into your lessons?
- What are some opportunities for students to solve problems, generate new ideas, and engage in other forms of creative thinking in your classroom?

#4: Set Goals

Friedrich Nietzsche said, "He who has a *why* to live for can bear almost any *how*."[3] Essentially, when we have deep underlying purpose fueling our work, the result is heightened work ethic and tenacity. This is why it is so important to help students learn to set meaningful goals that can become the fuel for their work. Students need to learn how to create these targets for themselves, and their teachers can help them do that.

Model Goal-Setting for Students   You probably have goals you are working toward. Whether it's a master's degree, paying off your home, saving up for a vacation, or so on, it can be beneficial to let students in on this process. Model for them what realistic goal-setting looks like. Let them know how you're working toward that goal and what small steps you are taking to get there.

For instance, I (Trevor) was once saving up to buy a newer car. I told my high school seniors that I wanted a Ford Fusion, but didn't have quite enough money to buy it yet. After laughing at me for wanting to get a Ford Fusion, they listened as I explained how I am setting aside a certain amount of money each month until I have what I need. Periodically I would check in with them and let them know where I was at with the goal. They knew when I hit different benchmarks because I let them in on a personal goal from my life.

And then on a cold day in December, when I pulled into the school parking lot with in a shiny pre-owned Ford Fusion with a pearl-white finish, the students clapped their hands, and we celebrated that I finally met my goal.

Jane Porter writes in her article "The Science of Setting and Achieving Goals," "Setting and achieving goals isn't about knowing how you'll get to the end result, but rather understanding the incremental steps needed to edge you closer to it."[4] Students need to see the journey that it takes to reach that achievement.

Teach Students to Practice Goal-Setting   As I was writing this chapter, my seven-year-old son asked what I was working on, and I said I'm writing about setting goals. He lit up and said, "That's what we're doing in class!" He went on to tell me that in his second-grade class, the teacher had students set a goal to become better readers. She explained to them that one of the best ways to do that is to re-read past texts that they may have struggled with the first time.

At the beginning of the week, she has students write their goals on sticky notes for how many times they will reread that week, and then has them put those sticky notes in a folder. Each time they chip away at that goal they remove one of the stickies from their folder. At the end of the week, if the sticky notes are no longer in their folder, they will know that they are now better readers.

My son's teacher is showing him at a very young age how to set goals and how to take part in incremental tasks to achieve them. This is a fundamental skill that my son will use the rest of his life.

A group of teachers at East Lee Alternative High School in Michigan planned a project to clean up the river that flows through their school's neighborhood. The teacher started the project by taking the students, who live in the inner city, on a field trip to the countryside where this river originates. Students made note of the differences between the river in the country versus the city: they saw how it is cleaner at its headwaters, its water is clearer, it has less pollution on the shoreline, and even has parks along the riverbank.

They began asking the question: Why isn't our part of the river like this?

Naturally, this motivated students to want to do something about the condition of the river by their homes. Their teacher had them set concrete goals to improve the river in their neighborhood. To create their goals, they answered questions like:

- How do you want the riverfront to look?
- What do you want the water quality to be?
- What does a plan look like to make these changes sustainable?
- How will we know if we are successful?

Once students could answer these questions, they could articulate the goals they had for this learning unit. The rest of the project was about achieving those goals. This entailed planning and brainstorming ideas. They had to present and fine-tune those ideas with each other. Students learned the science behind the river they are helping save, created materials using that knowledge to attract other people to help, and organized a cleanup event. At the end of the project, they held a huge community showcase that a county commissioner attended where students pitched their grand ideas.

That was their primary goal from the outset, and by the end of the project, they achieved it. And in the process, they learned science, persuasive writing, and the impact they can have when they work hard toward something meaningful.

The students achieved this goal because they cared about their neighborhood. My son achieved his goal because he cares about becoming a better reader. Students (and the rest of us) work harder and better when we know we're working toward something meaningful. So when teaching goal-setting, consider what is meaningful to your students, and help them articulate what their goal is and their plan to achieve it.

So, What about Boredom?   At the start of this chapter, we mentioned boredom. As new teachers, we both believed we had to be more entertaining than the cell phones in our students' pockets or the stars they see on TV. So we would have more breaks and use more transitions. We'd pack the class full of the most interesting information. We'd make class so entertaining that a video game or TV show would seem boring.

But here's the truth: we can't compete with a well-crafted TV show engineered for binge-watching. We can add badges and gamification, but we can't compete with a socially engineered video game designed to maximize user attention.

What we can offer is something different. Something authentic. Something human. Something that is occasionally boring or challenging or messy. When it comes to student engagement, you don't need to be more entertaining. Focus instead on community, relevance, and authenticity, and use these elements to increase students' attention and commitment levels. And sometimes this involves boredom.

The real change occurred when we abandoned the mindset of entertainment and shifted toward a mindset of authenticity (which we address in-depth in a future chapter). We recognized that authentic engagement often included moments of challenge, frustration, and even boredom.

Life is an adventure, and oftentimes, it is exciting and fun. However, doing taxes isn't exciting; it's actually quite boring. Filling up the gas tank is not very fun. Going to the doctor isn't fun. Cleaning your home, driving to work, doing laundry, and many other parts of life are not exactly stimulating, and yet, the mundane parts of life are necessary nonetheless.

The truth is: life can be boring.

And that's okay.

There are things we must do in-between those moments that are memorable and exciting, the things that make paying bills and taking your dog to the vet worth it. Of course, we want as many of these exciting, uplifting events in life as possible.

We want them in our classrooms too. However, students being constantly entertained in school sets unrealistic expectations for work and life. They need to know how to keep their minds and bodies activated when they are not captivated by the task in front of them. They need stamina, grittiness, endurance through the challenging and mundane. This stamina is developed through practice, and school is one of the places for that to happen.

But this is not the only reason to allow boredom to have a place in your classroom. A study published recently in the journal *Academy of Management Discoveries* had some participants take part in boredom-inducing tasks like sorting beans, then engage in a creative activity.[5] Researchers discovered those participants outperformed those who did not complete the boring task first on all creative tasks. Lack of stimulation actually stimulates creativity. It gives time for our minds to wander, work out problems, and create new ideas.

Researchers have repeatedly demonstrated this counterintuitive fact: boredom makes us more creative. Want to generate new ideas? Get bored. Want to think divergently? Make boredom a habit. In a distracted world, boredom is both a discipline and a gift.

Your students will benefit from moments in your class that are quiet, rote, and mundane. Constant stimulation, whether it be an exciting lesson, loud music, or time looking at screens releases dopamine in our brains. Dopamine is the euphoria hormone, and produces pleasure. However, constant hits of dopamine create a reliance on it, and we begin to crave more of it.[6]

When this happens, we miss out on the gift of boredom.

After learning this, I (Trevor) still played Weezer on Spotify while my students worked. I still convinced 14-year-olds to read their poetry at public open mic nights. You better believe I still talked like a character from *Braveheart* during class.

But I also had students sit in silence and research the history of South African diamond mines. And drilled in the concepts of simple and compound sentences. And gave assessments that let me know if they learned anything from our class time together. And sometimes, I sat down to grade papers while they silently read.

I let my students be bored.

I still used the techniques and practices we have discussed in this chapter to engage students, but reframed my motivation from entertainment to true engagement. I incorporated this into my new teacher mindset.

And it is often in these moments, where students push through the boredom because they know that what they are learning is meaningful and will have an impact on their lives, that I can sit back and be proud of the work that I am doing, even if it is sometimes a little boring.

Notes

1. Schlechty, P. C. (2002). *Working on the work: An action plan for teachers, principals, and superintendents*. The Jossey-Bass Education Series. Jossey-Bass.
2. Meyer, D. (2010, March). Math class needs a makeover [Video]. TED. https://www.ted.com/talks/dan_meyer_math_class_needs_a_makeover?language=en
3. Nietzsche, F. (1889). *Twilight of the idols*. (W. Kaufmann, Trans.). Random House.
4. Porter, Jane. Porter (2015). The science of setting and achieving goals. HelpScout. https://www.helpscout.com/blog/goal-setting/
5. Park, Guihyun, Lim, Beng-Chong Lim, and Oh, Hui Si Oh. (2019). Why being bored might not be a bad thing after all. *Academy of Management Discoveries*, 5(1): 78–92.
6. Mann, Sandi. (2017). *The science of boredom: The upside (and downside) of downtime*. Robinson.

Make Learning Authentic

One day when my (Trevor's) son was in second grade, he came home excited to tell me that he was doing a "project-based learning project" in his class. He hears his dad talk about project-based learning a lot, and knows some of my books are about PBL and hears me use the phrase all the time in Zoom calls and in conversation. I also had the chance to do some professional development on the subject with my son's teachers, so I was thrilled to hear it was being put into practice.

He told all about how his class is designing their "dream neighborhood." They're using math and shapes to design the buildings. While learning about maps, they will design their own for the neighborhood. In science, they'll learn about the plant life in their neighborhoods and the life cycles happening in that ecosystem. My son's teacher found lots of ways to tie in her class's content, and this sounded like a great project. So I asked, "And who is the neighborhood for?"

My eight-year-old replied, "What do you mean?"

I said, "When you're finished with the neighborhood, who are you presenting it to?"

Another way of asking this, perhaps to teachers, would be, "Who is your authentic audience? Whom from the real world can you produce work for that will amplify your engagement and make your work more real-world?"

I asked this because a key principle of project-based learning is authenticity and using the power of relevancy and personalization to heighten engagement (more on that in a minute). My understanding up to this point as a PBL teacher myself, as well as someone who trains teachers in it, is that *authentic* means "real-world." Students are not just engaged for their own growth, but are also causing change in the world around them.

This is why I was a little disappointed when my son told me they were just making their dream neighborhoods for the class. At the end of the project, his teacher said they would put all of their buildings together and everyone would talk about them. I thought to myself, "Wait, he's not presenting his design to an architect or a city planner? No real-world audience? There isn't even a showcase for parents to come and see their work?"

I smiled and nodded to my son, but in the back of mind I was thinking, *"His teacher clearly was not paying attention during my workshop."*

But then something strange happened. For the next two weeks, my son came home gushing about the project. He would excitedly tell me about designing the roofs of their houses and how strong triangles are for support. One night, he pulled out a ruler and showed me how to find the perimeter of an object, something he learned during this project. And I will never forget the day of the final presentation when he came home to proudly show me the building he designed for the neighborhood. By the end of this learning unit, my son not only was a better mathematician, scientist, and cartographer, he was also a better problem-solver and creative thinker. My son was hooked on this learning experience from start to finish.

Essentially, after this two-week project, I learned an invaluable lesson. I learned that my son's teacher knows her group of students much better than I do.

She knew that to a second-grade class, presenting a final design to your peers is just as authentic as presenting to an architect or panel of judges. His teacher didn't need to plan something to expand beyond the walls of the classroom to make this a real-world experience. Students were driven to work smart and hard because of the authenticity of this project. This taught me another valuable lesson as a teacher as well as a project-based learning instructor: authenticity is power *and* it can take on many forms.

What Makes Learning Authentic?

There is no single definition of *authentic learning* and no single learning task that will be authentic to every student at every moment. Authentic learning is what feels real and relevant to a student in the moment.

That's it.

Authentic learning doesn't have to be a massive project. It could be a 5-minute show-and-tell activity, a 15-minute free read, or a Socratic Seminar. It could be a writing assignment that explores their unique interests or an actual marketing campaign for a real company.

The point is that student engagement is no longer driven solely by the traditional motivators: grades, parent pressure, or even student advancement in a course or school. Of course, these motivators work for some students. A percentage of the population either cares about grades, or at least, cares about the consequences of bad ones. But what about the students who do not? Or what about the "high-achieving" students who have mastered the education system well enough to earn good grades without having to actually learn the material?

With authentic work, now all students have the opportunity to engage in inspired work. When teachers can find ways to make learning authentic for students, engagement and learning retention heightens. In his article "Service-Learning and Academic Success: The Links to Retention Research," Dan Simonet uncovers research that shows when students are engaged in purposeful, authentic work, they experience measurable growth in social, behavioral, emotional, and cognitive development.[1] Essentially, when their work has an authentic purpose, when they know it is authentic and impactful, they learn to collaborate better, are better behaved, emotionally mature, and they learn content at a deeper level.

Authenticity in school work drives more student engagement and impactful learning. In this chapter, we will explore different ways we can design authentic learning experiences to achieve true student engagement.

Authentic Problems

When I taught eighth grade, every student had to complete a workbook designed to prepare them for the standardized test at the end of the quarter. One section was on the Pythagorean theorem.

"This doesn't make any sense," a student pointed out.

"Can you explain what part is confusing?" I asked.

"The whole thing," he responded. I quietly read the problem about a baseball catcher who needed to use the Pythagorean theorem to figure out the distance from home plate to second base before throwing out a runner.

"What's wrong with it?" I asked.

"It's a stupid problem. I mean, what catcher is going to use the Pythagorean theorem in a game. No one would actually do that."

He had a point. In an attempt at making math relevant, the problem in this workbook was an example of what Dan Meyer refers to as pseudo-context.[2] It's what happens when students use math in a way that doesn't actually reflect any genuine context.

Sure you can use the Pythagorean theorem to figure out that distance, *but who would ever actually do that?*

Students are less engaged when they solve irrelevant and inauthentic problems. They begin to view the subject as irrelevant—merely another hoop to jump through on the journey toward college. Kids are naturally driven to solve problems. But when we root it into pseudo-context, they grow less curious and they lose interest in the subject.

By contrast, authentic problems pull students into a subject in a way that piques their curiosity and fuels their desire to learn more.

One of the ways to incorporate authentic problem-solving is through PBL. The idea here is to present students with an authentic problem or challenge that they must solve. The grade or even learning the content is no longer the primary motivator for students; instead, it's solving a problem typically rooted in a real-world context.

The Four Phases of Problem-Based Learning

Problem-based learning can be broken down into four phases (see Figure 9.1). The first phase is about identifying the problem. The problem can be a hypothetical scenario that takes students a day or two to answer, or sometimes the problem is expansive enough to encompass an entire learning unit. Sometimes the teacher decides on the problem, or in other cases, individual students or the entire classroom community presents the initial problem.

In phase two, students develop a plan for solving the problem. Here, students work independently or collaboratively brainstorming solutions.

The next phase is the implementation of the plan. In this phase, students test their plan to see if they can solve the problem.

Then finally, they move to the last phase where they evaluate the implementation. Here, students analyze the results and they also reflect on the process.

Problem-based learning works best when students solve real-world problems. It's important that the problems feel real to the students, that it is not just applicable, but authentic.

Authentic Projects

Like problem-based learning, project-based learning is also about solving a problem, only now there is a culminating event at the end of the experience. Throughout

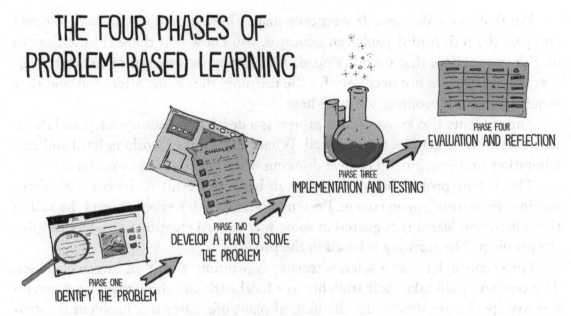

THE FOUR PHASES OF PROBLEM-BASED LEARNING

PHASE FOUR
EVALUATION AND REFLECTION

PHASE THREE
IMPLEMENTATION AND TESTING

PHASE TWO
DEVELOP A PLAN TO SOLVE THE PROBLEM

PHASE ONE
IDENTIFY THE PROBLEM

FIGURE 9.1 The four phases of problem-based learning.

the learning unit, students create some sort of product as a solution to the problem. What differentiates this from the traditional experience of doing projects in school is that with project-based learning, the project is present throughout the entire learning unit. It is not something that is given to students after they learn the material, but instead, is what drives their learning of it.

Think about it like the main course of a meal and the dessert.

Desserts come after the meal. Sometimes it's nice to order a dessert, but you don't need it. You need the main course; that's where you get your necessary vitamins and sustenance. It's often like this with school projects: first comes the direct instruction, discussion, worksheets, and so on, the main course, and then comes the project.

> *We're going to learn all about volcanoes and how they're formed and igneous rock and tectonic plates, you'll take a test, then you're going to get into a group to create a model volcano.*

Sound familiar?

We don't *need* desserts. If we never made these model volcanoes, we could still pass the test. And if you're an educator, you know that there is little time to do things in school that we don't need. This is why we often want to avoid projects because they're not necessary for the learning; they come afterward, and they require time and resources we don't have.

And students also know when a project is a dessert and unnecessary, and this is why they often don't like them as well. What's the point of working hard and collaborating, and engaging in critical thinking when it's not even important?

This is why project-based learning can be so powerful. At its core, it's about making the learning main course. Present students with a problem, and then all of the subsequent learning is geared in some way toward creating a product to solve the problem. The learning is based in the project.

For instance, let's say a science teacher is planning a unit on invasive species. The teacher could take their students to a local park and show them how certain invasive species are destroying the natural plant life. After this problem is introduced, the project is about solving it. To do so, students could create public service announcement (PSA) videos, education materials for the community, or even plan an event where community members show up to pull invasive species from that park.

To complete a project like this, not only will students need to learn about invasive species (academic content), they will have to exercise the essential skills to complete the authentic task. They will have to work in groups (collaboration), come up with solutions (critical thinking), create materials (creativity), present their learning (communication), and so on. This is the power of giving students authentic work. Because the students are completing a meaningful project, they learn the content at a deeper level as well as develop these essential skills.

Authentic Research

Problem- and project-based learning often begin with a quality teacher-generated authentic problem. However, we also want students to ask their own questions and find the answers through an authentic research experience. Authentic research isn't merely a language arts idea. It's what happens in any subject area where students can ask their own questions and seek out their own answers. It might involve a Wonder Day activity in social studies, where students ask any question they want about the subject area and then gather information from multiple sources. By contrast, in science, it might look more like an independent science experiment, similar to that of a Science Fair Project. In an art class, it might resemble a curation project, where students explore various artists, genres, and time periods.

Authentic research involves connecting to information with authentic source material. This might involve interviewing an entomologist in a second-grade science lesson on insects or encouraging a high-school history student to interview a firsthand witness of genocide. It might involve an exploration of older primary source materials, a review of data, or an exploration of a story. Students might conduct interviews or surveys, and analyze the data. They might do observations or engage in hands-on, play-based research.

One option for authentic research is to implement an inquiry-based learning activity.

The inquiry process is a cycle beginning with a provocation or core idea that sparks students' curiosity. This helps activate their prior knowledge. Students then ask questions, which spark their research. In this research phase, they might engage in interviews, find online sources, or conduct an experiment. This leads to a phase where students analyze data or organize their information and draw key conclusions. From here, they communicate their answers with a larger audience and reflect on their learning. This often works as a new provocation, which leads to new questions.

Authentic Interests

Earlier, we mentioned the baseball word problem with the catcher and the Pythagorean theorem. This scenario didn't work because it failed to connect the subject matter to the students' interest. Instead, it was like the interest (baseball) stood apart from the subject (math), even though the author of the problem attempted to link them together. The problem could probably use a little tweaking, but the author was probably moving in the right direction. Students often engage more when the links between their interests and the subject matter are authentic.

Math becomes more authentic if we ask the question, "Are sequels actually a good financial decision?" or "Should movie theaters reduce the cost of candy?" Baseball grows far more interesting when asking, "Is on-base percentage plus slugging (OPS) or batting average a better metric for a hitter?" In each of these cases, students are using math as a tool for understanding a topic they care about rather than solving math problems that don't actually allow students to learn anything deeper about topics that interest them.

We can also create spaces where students can pursue their interests within the confines of the subject matter. By choosing topic-neutral standards, students can learn whatever topic they like as they practice content-related skills. Here are a few examples:

- Students do a show-and-tell activity where they bring in an item that represents their culture in social studies.

- Students document examples of environmental text around their world in reading.

- Students start a blog on whatever topic they choose while they practice reading, researching, and writing in language arts.

- Students create how-to videos on some type of skill or hobby they have in a functional writing unit in language arts.

- Students practice social studies methods standards (how to make a timeline, how to read primary sources, etc.) as they do a "History of _____" project on any topic they like.

- After going to the library, students have silent reading time where they can read any novel they choose. You will discuss and assess the same themes, motifs, and elements of story with them, but they can choose the text they will learn from.

- Students engage in a Genius Hour project for the entire school year. Each Friday, they have designated time to work on an individual project relating to something they care about.

Authentic Audience

Traditionally in school, students turn in their work for their teachers and no one else. It might end up in a backpack or maybe on the classroom walls, but the teacher is the primary audience.

And that's often okay. Most work should be private. However, at some point, we want students to share their work with a larger audience.

When this happens, students work harder because the work has a deeper meaning. There's higher engagement because students can see the connection between the learning and their world. Class becomes less about preparing for the real world and instead is about engaging in it. Students often grow more empathetic as they think about their audience and whom they're serving, and can gain new perspectives from professionals outside of the school setting.

Having an authentic audience helps provide context to what students are learning. By having your students present their work at the end of a learning unit to someone other than you, you are helping them see that learning does not happen inside a vacuum. Instead, it is something that helps us solve real problems for real people.

When designing a learning unit or converting an existing one to an authentic project, one of the key questions to ask is: "Who is using this content in the real world?" From there, it's just a matter of inviting them to be an audience to your students' work. This may be an expert in their field who you ask to come and evaluate what your students create; maybe it's a showcase for community members who are also affected by the problem students are solving. Or like the example I gave earlier with my son's second grade class, it may just be other students.

Note that an authentic audience is not always the widest audience available. If a student pours their heart out into a writing piece that they choose to keep private, it can still be authentic. Sometimes an audience of one is the most authentic choice. Similarly, I have had students give powerful presentations to a small group of fellow students and it felt authentic to every person who was present. And on the other end of the spectrum, I've had students create work for organizations and businesses that were, before this project, completely unconnected to our school.

The key element here is authenticity. Does it feel authentic to the students when they share it with others? Here are some potential authentic audiences:

- **Showcase:** An event or presentation where students publicly demonstrate and share the outcomes of their projects with a wider audience.

- **Administration:** Invite your school and district leaders to observe and evaluate student work.

- **Public officials:** Invite leaders in your community and state to serve as an authentic audience. (Note: You might be surprised how willing they often are to connect with schools. Your students offer fresh perspectives and this is great PR!)

- **Event**: Students help plan an event as an authentic outcome for a project.

- **Other students:** Presenting work to your peers is one of the most powerful authentic audiences.

- **Digital publishing:** Use social media, video sharing, platforms, blogs, newspapers, or any other digital location to display student work.

- **Themselves:** Students create from intrinsic motivation.

Finding Authentic Partners

For over 10 years, I (Trevor) have been leading workshops for teachers on how to plan project-based learning projects, and at every single one, I ask if anyone knows someone who is connected with their local zoo. At every workshop for a decade, at least one person raises their hand and shares a connection they have with someone at the zoo. Literally, every single time. I then make the point that if you want to plan a project that has something to do with animals, and you're looking for an authentic audience, all you have to do is ask a group of teachers and someone will be able to connect you with the zoo!

The point is: we all have networks. When coming up with authentic ideas, we need to take advantage of that. Do you want your students to present to an official in local government? Someone in your circle probably knows someone in government whom your students can connect with. Would bringing in a pilot enhance a physics unit? I'm guessing you, at least, know someone who knows a pilot who could work with your class. Reaching out to friends, family, parents, and colleagues to ask for help is a great way to come up with ideas and increase authenticity in your classroom.

Authentic Play

Spend an hour with a toddler and you'll notice a constant sense of wonder and curiosity. They are always asking, always imagining, always creating, and always learning. This leads to toddlers experiencing more brain development than any other time in their lives. And most of the time, this happens while they play. Or another way of putting it, they wonder, imagine, create, and learn while they are enjoying themselves.

Mr. (Fred) Rogers said, "Play is often talked about as if it were a relief from serious learning. But for children, play is serious learning. Play is really the work of childhood." Essentially, play is as authentic as it gets for children.

Far too often, school is a place that restricts play more than it promotes it. From decreasing recess time to increasing standardized testing to dwindling resources being allocated to PE and the arts to the simple fact that the vast majority of secondary-age students do not receive any unstructured playtime throughout their day, many students do not get to play enough at school.

This is a problem. Play can lead to better emotional regulation and executive function. It can help us build empathy and interpersonal skills. Play can improve divergent thinking and creativity. It's why so many of the best problem-solvers tend to engage in play-based excursions. Play can help learning stick because the concepts connect to an immersive experience with heightened emotions. This, in turn, helps move information from working memory to short-term memory to long-term memory.

Also, play is about joy, and why wouldn't we want more joy for our students? Play is essential to human beings, and we learn and grow more because of it.

However, you probably don't have a say about how much recess your students receive, what is assessed on standardized tests, or how much funding goes to the arts. There will always be systemic factors beyond your control. But you can find opportunities to incorporate play into the everyday work students do.

At a younger level, we might incorporate play by having students spend extended time engaging in imaginative play around a story they're reading. We might ask students to play with three-dimensional objects and identify examples from around the room before learning about three-dimensional objects in direct instruction. Play bingo to review concepts, build model volcanoes, use vinegar to turn eggs to rubber, taste foods from different cultures, have a dance everyone does at the beginning of the day, do a scavenger hunt, have a dress-up day after finishing a unit, have an instrument petting zoo in music, find ways to make learning sillier and more joyful.

At an older level, it's the same thing, just adjusted to the interests of your students. Ask students to engage in role-playing games as they build empathy in a design-thinking challenge. Or have them use math skills to design an escape room for their friends to play. Or have them do a simulation, conduct class outside when it's nice out, act out *Romeo and Juliet*, hold a debate, play music while they work, plant a garden, write music, tell stories, quiz with Kahoot, solve puzzles—you get the point.

Sometimes these small injections of joy in the classroom experience can have a massive effect on the way students learn and engage.

Authentic Discussion

Authentic learning involves authentic conversations. Some of these are open-ended small-group discussions. Others are highly structured mock trials or debates. Some are low-tech Socratic discussions where students put their technology away. Others are online chats they participate in, podcasts they record, or annotations they leave on a shared document. Some of these conversations connect to current events and real-world contexts, but others might relate to a fictional world rooted in fantasy. The underlying common thread, though, is that students engage in inherently meaningful, authentic conversations.

Now, it's one thing to recognize the value of holding authentic conversations and discussions with students; it's another getting students to meaningfully engage in them. Few things are as frustrating as planning on a rich and dynamic discussion, only to ask the first prompt and hear nothing but crickets. So here are a few suggestions to engage students in class discussion.

Create a Safe Environment   Having a safe environment for discussion is crucial because speaking up takes courage. Whether you are a child in a kindergarten classroom or a teacher sitting in a staff meeting, sharing your thoughts with others requires vulnerability and bravery. So when students are learning a vital skill, we have to do everything we can to make the space one in which all students feel like they can take risks. It involves creating an environment where everyone's contributions are valued and respected, regardless of their background or status. Every participant should feel heard and understood.

This begins with articulating the expectations and realities of discussion. Here's what I mean by that. Discussion usually entails sharing undeveloped, unrefined ideas. They're not polished. When you discuss, you are not giving a speech. The discussion is more the rough draft rather than the final one. So we have to let students know they're not expected to be completely clear in sharing their thoughts or phrase everything perfectly. It sounds simple, but students need to know they have permission to try to put together whatever is swirling around in their heads without being rejected or shamed.

One way to help curb some of that rejection is to have ground rules for discussion in your classroom, a set of unwavering standards that everyone in the room, students and teacher, must abide by when discussion is taking place.

And one of the ways to really increase the effectiveness of these rules is to create them alongside your students. Do this by simply asking them what guidelines should be followed during class discussion. Here's an example of what the ground rules can look like:

- Listen respectfully when someone else is talking.
- Be critical of ideas, not people.
- Allow everyone a chance to speak.
- Ask for clarification if you are confused.
- Always work toward a shared understanding.
- Collaborate, don't compete.
- If you are offended by something, call it out immediately.

The ground rules are non-negotiable. Part of your role in facilitating discussion is ensuring they are followed, and that you follow them to keep the discussion environment safe.

Student-Owned Discussion   When students control a discussion and guide it in the direction they desire, they become significantly more invested than when the teacher maintains complete control. One way to give away that control is having students create the discussion prompts. What if, instead of having students read a chapter and providing answers, they read the chapter and formulate questions that will be used to discuss their learning?

Or you could put kids in groups and tell them, "In 10 minutes, we're going to have a class discussion. So in your groups, develop three questions on the subject matter, and we are going to put those questions in a hat, draw from them and let that lead our discussion."

This not only gets students thinking deeper about the material before discussion, they also feel ownership over that discussion when it's taking place.

Another effective approach to empower students is assigning specific roles during the discussion, ensuring that every student has an opportunity to contribute and take ownership of the process. These roles could include:

- **First Speaker:** Initiates the discussion by responding to the prompt first.

- **Timekeeper:** Monitors and manages the group's allotted discussion time.

- **Reporter:** Summarizes the small group discussion's key points to the larger class at the end.

- **Facilitator:** Helps the discussion by periodically summarizing what's being said and synthesizing the main ideas at the conclusion.

- **Equity Monitor:** Encourages all members to share their ideas, focusing on ensuring that everyone's voice is heard.

- **Alternative Advocate:** Plays the role of Devil's Advocate throughout the discussion, consistently proposing alternative points of view to challenge the ideas being discussed.

Assigning these roles can motivate students who might otherwise hesitate to participate in the discussion. Moreover, when students have specific roles to fulfill, they often feel more comfortable sharing their thoughts and ideas.

Use Different Discussion Strategies   The final major component for a strong class discussion is employing a variety of strategies to engage all your students. We'll share a few of our favorite strategies here, but know that we are just scratching the surface and there are many other effective strategies available. Consider utilizing various discussion strategies as akin to taking different routes to reach the same destination. For some of your students, certain routes may be more effective than others. Therefore, by offering different routes, you increase the likelihood that everyone will reach the destination. In essence, by employing different discussion strategies, you help engage all students in authentic discussions.

The Socratic Seminar

Socratic Seminars are where participants engage in thoughtful dialogue to explore complex ideas, texts, or issues. At their core, they are student-centered and student-led. While Socratic Circles can take on different forms, here are some key components:

1. Students sit in a circle asking and answering questions while the teacher remains silent.

2. The discussion is free-flowing. There is no raising of hands or calling on names.

3. The best discussions are explanatory and open rather than cut-and-dried debates. While a question might lead to persuasive thought, the goal should be to examine points of view and construct deeper meaning.

A variation of the Socratic Seminar includes the Fish Bowl Approach, where you arrange the chairs in an inner circle and an outer circle. The students on the outside will take notes while the students on the inside engage in the Socratic Seminar.

Conver-Stations

This discussion strategy, inspired by educator Sarah Brown Wessling,[3] arranges students into groups of four to six members, each assigned a discussion question. As previously mentioned, students can generate these questions before the activity. After several minutes of discussion or until the conversation matures, two individuals from each group should switch to a different group while the others remain.

With the rotations, the discussion continues, integrating the newcomers who contribute insights from their previous group's conversation. These rotations can repeat as needed, invigorating conversations with fresh perspectives and ideas. Students take full ownership of the discussion, while teachers can freely move around the room, engaging and contributing as they see fit.

Write, Pair, Share

One of the problems with leading a full-class discussion is that students are having to process and share information with everyone else on the spot. This requires immense vulnerability, and many students are not willing to go there, hence the crickets. With Write, Pair, Share, students first process by themselves, writing down key ideas that they will then discuss. After a minute or two of writing, students find a partner and share the thoughts they just wrote.

The short bit of writing helps students do two important things. First, they are processing the information in a kinesthetic form, transferring their thoughts to words. This deepens the learning even before discussion. The writing also gives them a road map for the following discussion, which builds confidence for sharing their thinking with someone else. This confidence almost always leads to better discussion versus jumping right into the pairing and sharing.

Checklist: Authenticity Audit

Use the following questions to do an authenticity audit of a unit plan.

- Relevance:
  - Does the learning task connect to real-world situations or issues?

- Can students see the immediate or future relevance of the task in their lives?
- Does the learning task tap into students' personal experiences and backgrounds?
- Student Choice:
  - Are there opportunities for students to make choices within the learning experience?
  - Can students personalize aspects of the task based on their interests?
- Problem-Solving:
  - Does the task require critical thinking and problem-solving skills?
  - Are students challenged to explore solutions rather than follow a prescribed path?
- Collaboration:
  - Does the learning experience involve collaboration with peers or external entities?
  - Are students encouraged to share ideas and work together toward a common goal?
- Authentic Assessment:
  - Are assessment methods aligned with real-world expectations and standards?
  - Do assessments reflect the complexity and authenticity of the learning task?
- Reflection:
  - Is there a structured reflection component within the learning experience?
  - Do students have opportunities to think about their learning process and outcomes?
- Varied Learning Formats:
  - Are there diverse ways for students to demonstrate understanding (e.g., projects, discussions, presentations)?
  - Does the learning experience cater to different learning styles and preferences?
- Integration of Technology:
  - Does technology play a role in enhancing the authenticity of the learning task?
  - Are students using tools and platforms relevant to the real-world context?

- Connection to Community:
  - Does the learning experience involve interactions with the local community or experts in the field?
  - Can students see the broader impact or implications of their work beyond the classroom?
- Flexibility and Adaptability:
  - Can the learning task be adapted based on the evolving interests and needs of students?
  - Is there room for unexpected discoveries and detours within the learning process?

Notes

1. Simonet, D. (2008, May). *Service-learning and academic success: The links to retention research.* Minnesota Campus Compact.
2. Meyer, Dan. (2010). Pseudocontext Saturdays: Introduction. dy/dan. http://blog.mrmeyer.com/2010/pseudocontext-saturdays-introduction/
3. Teaching Channel. (n.d.). Conver-stations strategy [Video file]. Retrieved from https://learn.teachingchannel.com/video/conver-stations-strategy

Navigating the Constantly Evolving Technological Landscape

Every one of us walks around holding miniature supercomputers completing tasks that once seemed inconceivable. As a kid, if I wanted to look up an article, I had to go to the library and search a card catalogue only to navigate the dark art of microfiche. Taking a photo meant carrying a roll of film to the drug store and waiting a few days to get it back. In high school, we used to use the term *information superhighway* to describe being online.

Fast-forward a few decades and my daughter walks into the room with an iPad. "Dad, you have to play this new game called Crossy Road."

I play it for a minute before responding, "I'm pretty sure this is Frogger with a new name."

When I began teaching, most educators used transparency projectors and had marker-stained fingertips. People still called handouts and worksheets "dittos." We were excited when the final classrooms in our wing converted from chalkboards to whiteboards. Over the next decade, I converted old boxy computers into Linux machines so students could use shared documents and engage in blogging. I received an interactive whiteboard and a set of digital cameras. A few years later, we had netbooks, and later, laptops. When smartphones grew in popularity, students could finally record podcasts and film documentaries on the go. But I also struggled with the challenge of incessant distractions from apps vying for my students' attention.

Now, smartphones are no longer novel. In fact, we now just call them "phones." Many new teachers grew up with this technology. But as you enter the classroom, new emerging technologies will continue to change the world.

Right now, we are in the midst of a machine learning revolution. With generative AI, it is easier than ever to create content in a matter of seconds. Teachers are grappling with what this means for creativity and academic integrity. They're wrestling with what these changes will mean for our students as they graduate and enter the quickly evolving workforce. But they're also finding creative ways to use generative AI to differentiate instruction, design resources, and manage their workload professionally.

None of us can adequately predict what these changes will mean for the classroom. For this reason, we won't share ideas for specific apps and programs you should use. Instead, our goal is to think strategically about how we approach technology. Having a New Teacher Mindset recognizes that technology will continue to have a disruptive impact on education. In some cases, these disruptions will cause damage. In some cases, they will lead to new opportunities. But, as teachers, we can be adaptable with new technologies and focus on the learning rather than the tech. From there, we can ask, "What does it mean to use it wisely?"

Focus on the Learning, Not the Technology

Technology can create amazing opportunities for deeper learning. The connective and creative capacity of our tools means we can do things more quickly and feasibly than ever before. We can design solutions, connect with experts, engage in simulations, and analyze data in a way that was once cost prohibitive and labor intensive. However, if we're not careful, the tools can drive the learning experiences. This is why it helps to start with your learning targets and then focus on ways the technology can either enhance or transform the learning experience. As you explore the available technology, consider the following questions:

1. **Will You Receive Proper Training before Implementation?**

   Far too often, schools spend their budget on a new tech tool, only to have no money left over to train teachers in that tool. Therefore, teachers are expected to use their limited-if-any planning time, or time before or after school, to figure it out. I (Trevor) was once told by district administration to use a new multi-million–dollar software to track student success in my classes. Great, will do.

   But when I used the program, it was like trying to read hieroglyphics. I had no idea how to navigate the software, make changes, or even access the homepage. After many frustrating afternoons and what ended up being wasted time, I gave up. I stopped using it. So did the rest of the teaching staff, and the software was soon abandoned. I can only imagine how many books I could have purchased for my classroom library with the money wasted on that software.

   The idea for the tech was great, and I'm sure it would've been effective if we knew how to use it, but there was no training. So when researching tech, find out if there is adequate training. If assigned new technology, ask if training will be provided.

2. Does the Technology Increase Student Engagement?

One of the key indicators for student success is student engagement. A highly engaged student is one who is eager to learn and grow. Technology in the classroom should serve the purpose of engaging students. This is one of the reasons some would advocate the usage of cell phones in class. Because students like being on their phones, why not take advantage of that and use them during instruction?

I couldn't agree more!

But what often happens is that the phones lead to distraction and therefore disengage students from the learning experience. There needs to be structure around the use of phones, and processes to ensure they engage students in the learning and not in social media. This goes for any ed tech tool. Does it engage students? Is it actually enhancing their learning or distracting them from it?

3. Does the Technology Teach Transferable Skills?

Let's be honest, most of our students will never see a three-dimensional printer after high school. Most will never edit a video using Adobe Premiere, nor will they use Google Tour Creator to map out their own museum. So if the purpose of teaching students to use these tools is just for them to learn how to use these tools, after graduation that information will be obsolete to them.

However, if by using these tools students learn new skills that they can use throughout their lives, then the tool serves a purpose. For instance, while most students may not become video editors, video editing is a great way to organize visual information and put it in an understandable sequence. From being a teacher, salesperson, or scientist, this skill applies far beyond video editing. Using an engaging video editing program can be a great way to teach students this skill. But again, if students learn and use this tool for the sole purpose of editing videos without highlighting the bigger picture, then it would not pass the litmus test for being allowed in the classroom.

4. Will the Technology Make Your Life Easier?

Teachers perform time-consuming work with limited resources every day. From designing lessons to classroom management, the work is hard and complex. Tech should not be adding to the workload but instead should be lessening it in some way. Of course, with any new technology, there is a learning curve and a time sacrifice required, but at some point, the new technology should no longer be frustrating.

And I mean not frustrating at all. If an entire staff of teachers does not like a grading app that they are required to use for whatever reason, then the app needs to be improved by the company or the school should find a better one. There is no time for ineffective technology. Developers need to receive pushback and make their products work for the specific people who are actually using them.

5. What Technology Fits Best with My Students?

K–3 students might work best on tablets and using apps that have a simpler interface. By contrast, high school students often perform better on computers where they can perform more complex tasks. Make sure that the technology you use is developmentally appropriate. Ultimately, you know your classroom context the best.

6. Does the Technology Adhere to School and District Policies?

Here in the United States, we have Children's Internet Protection Act (CIPA) and Children's Online Privacy Protection Act (COPPA) laws that dictate key information about student privacy. Some of the great tools that we might use in other industries are not compliant at the K–12 level.

7. What Is the *Actual* Cost of Using the Technology?

We expect technology to have a financial cost. However, technology can be time-consuming as well. This is especially true with some of the most robust and complex software. There's also a potential for a social or personal cost. I remember going full-force into technology and realizing that I wasn't asking students to speak face to face. I wasn't incorporating movement into my lessons. They worked collaboratively on screen, but they were missing the vital element of being present with their groups. So, I had to rethink the social cost of the technology and focus on incorporating some of the lo-fi, low-tech elements.

Setting Expectations with Technology

Furthermore, it's important to go over expectations with technology. If a student views technology as a method of entertainment, you might need to help them make that paradigm shift toward viewing it as a learning tool. You will likely need to cover expectations for using the technology responsibly, including how to manage the physical hardware. In addition, you might want to embed digital citizenship mini-lessons into the technology integration. For example, you might get into digital footprint and respect online when having students share their work with an audience. This is also a great time to embed elements of media literacy as they engage in online research.

In previous chapters, we explored how to empower students to help create rituals and norms. The same is true with technology. Students should engage in a meaningful dialogue about acceptable use. You can guide students through this discussion, asking what expectations the class should hold for each of the following headings:

- Behavior:
  - Potential discussion points: Treat people the way you want to be treated. Show forgiveness and empathy when people make mistakes. Avoid insulting others.

- Language:
  - Potential discussion points: Use language to build people up instead of tear down people. Express yourself clearly using complete sentences.

- Listening:
  - Potential discussion points: Listen to others all the way before making a judgment.

- Friendships:
  - Potential discussion points: Make sure you know people before making "friends" online. Avoid making friends with random strangers.

- Permission:
  - Potential discussion points: Ask people before you take a picture, post a picture. or write an update about them.

- Creating:
  - Potential discussion points: Be creative online. Make sure that what you post is your own. Use the Creative Commons when posting pictures or resources. Add to the Creative Commons. Avoid plagiarism.

- Appropriate:
  - Potential discussion points: Make sure that you post things that are true, kind, helpful, and necessary. Don't post anything that would embarrass you or others.

The Constantly Changing Tides of Technology

In the 1970s, when calculators started to become widespread, they were banned in most schools. And yet, in 1975, calculators were in one in nine American homes; meaning, schools could ban them all they wanted, but they were still being used at home to solve math problems. And within a decade, the College Board was mandating their use on the AP Exam, and by 1990, they were being used in every school in the country.

This wasn't just the result of educators throwing up their hands and saying, "If you can't beat 'em, join 'em." No, if you look at this history, you'll see it's because educators realized students can do more complex math with the use of a calculator. But educators first had to figure out how to take advantage of that technology.

Artificial Intelligence (AI)

Generative AI seemingly appeared out of nowhere, rattling the world with its powerful capabilities. Within the digital realm, it conjures lifelike prose, generates art that mimics human strokes, and composes melodies that resonate with the soul—blurring the lines between creator and creation. The rapid advancement of AI continues to astonish, promising a future where it might simulate human experiences and revolutionize industries we never thought possible.

It can also write five-paragraph essays in the tone and style of seventh graders, and solve complex math problems in a matter of seconds, and will even show its work.

Upon the release of AI into the mainstream, much of the conversation in the education world has been about how to prevent cheating. Of course, students can use this technology to cheat. That is a very real concern that educators need to be aware of. However, if we focus only on surveillance and "catching" cheating, we will likely end up in a never-ending game of cat and mouse.

The truth is, these tools can make life easier, so whether they are prohibited or not, students will use them in school or as soon as they get home.

Just like the use of calculators in the 1970s.

This should cause us to consider what kind of assignments we give students. Writing prompts need to have a critical thinking element to them, requiring more than a regurgitation of information. If students can just plug in a prompt that will generate them an essay, then the assignment probably needs some reworking. For instance, instead of assigning an essay asking students to describe the five causes of World War I, perhaps give the prompt "How do the causes of World War I relate to a current conflict in the world today?"

Or, beyond critical thinking, give students assignments that are personal and reflective. Ask how a subject connects or relates to their own lives, something AI cannot do for them. Teaching geography? Instead of asking students to just write about how rivers form, ask how that geographic formation has affected their lives in some way. Now students are having to connect the content to their own personal experiences. Of course, AI can still assist them to write the general content portion, but in adding a personal element they are now forced to understand the content.

The truth is, while alarming and even a little scary, AI is a powerful tool. Of course, it raises questions around ethics and responsibility, and these are discussions teachers need to have with their students. But it is also a time-saver, an idea generator, information gatherer, summarizer, researcher, spell checker, problem-solver, software designer, and so on. Instead of rejecting this tool because of its negative potential, we need to find ways to embrace it. Because AI isn't going anywhere, and if students don't learn how to use it appropriately and effectively in school, they might not learn how to elsewhere.

As educators, we constantly face significant challenges with disruptive technologies. But adapting to them and allowing positive disruption is not just the educator's task. We won't be able to rely on a simple set of policies when the technology continues to change at a rapid pace. Instead, we will need to empower students to think critically about the way they use new technology and help them shift their mindset as well.

Using AI Ethically and Responsibly

With generative AI, students will find it easier than ever to cheat on an essay. But it can also be a powerful tool for problem-solving. Students can use generative AI to answer questions and build conceptual knowledge. They can use these tools to create scaffolds and supports and thus increase accessibility. We, as teachers, can craft learning opportunities where students discover what it means to have a human-centered approach to using AI.

Access the Digital Download Using AI in Writing at newteachermindset.com.

Knowing how to use a tool isn't enough. We need students to reflect on the ethical use of technology as well. As we move forward with new emerging technologies, our students will need to wrestle with hard questions. In the case of AI, students might ask:

- When is it my voice and when is it the voice of AI? When am I giving away too much of my own thinking to a machine?
- What do I gain and lose from using machine learning?
- How do I think ethically about the ways that generative AI will change the world?
- How do I think critically about information in an age of AI and deep fakes?

This approach is at the heart of authentic blended learning. It is the overlap of the human element and the machine element. Whether you are in-person, teaching an online course, running a hybrid system, or in a distance learning situation (due to an emergency like a snow day), you are constantly navigating the intersection of the human element and the online world. So, how do we ensure that students are leveraging the full creative and connective capacity of these tools?

Leverage the Creative Capacity of Our Tools

In education, we often use consumer language to describe instruction. How do you deliver the lesson? Did the students get it? What grade did they earn? And there is some truth to this. We need to engage in direct instruction. We often model a particular skill that students then copy. Other times, we help students attain knowledge by reading articles, watching videos, or listening to lectures.

This is especially common in online courses, where the predominant model is to consume content and then discuss the information afterward.

However, at some point, we want students to engage with technology in meaningful, creative ways. We want them to be problem-solvers and makers and designers. In other words, we want students to develop a maker mindset. This is why, ultimately, they need to engage in creative work online. But what does this actually look like?

- **Blogging:** Thematic blogs are blogs based on a student's interests, passions, and ideas. It could be a foodie blog, a sports blog, a fashion blog, a science blog, or a history blog. They choose the topic and the audience. It's a great way for students to practice writing in different genres (persuasive, functional, informational/expository, narrative) with specific blog topics they choose. They can also add multimedia components, like slideshows, pictures, videos, and audio.

- **Podcasting:** With podcasts, students create audio recordings that they then share with an authentic audience. They can work individually, with partners, or in small groups. It can be more scripted or more open. If you want, you can have students edit the podcasts and add music by using GarageBand or Audacity. But you can also do a simple recording with phones.

- **Videos:** Video creation is a little more complicated. It is often more time-consuming and sometimes requires additional skills. However, if students are at home, they might just be willing to spend the additional time creating a video. A simple option for video creation is an annotated slideshow. Here, students create a slideshow and then record the audio as they move through it. They can do this on PowerPoint, Keynote, or Google Slides.

- **Virtual music or audio composition:** Use online music creation platforms that allow students to compose, edit, and share their music or audio compositions.

- **Animation projects:** There are many animation tools you can introduce to students, allowing them to create animated shorts or presentations.

- **Social media campaigns:** Have students design and execute creative social media campaigns on topics related to your class. They could advocate for a change they want to see, raise awareness about a certain topic, or simply spread joy to others.

Notice that none of these are new ideas. Thirty years ago, students had the ability to create videos or record audio. However, those required massive studios with expensive equipment. The technology has simply made it faster, easier, and cheaper. As we move into an era of AI, we will likely see a proliferation of editing software that will reduce the time-wasting tedium of video and audio editing, meaning students will have more time to focus on the human elements of videos and podcasts.

Leverage the Connective Capacity of Our Tools

We live in a world where there are countless online tools for communication and collaboration. We can send instant messages, edit on a shared paper in Google Docs, hop onto a video conference, and easily send files back and forth. And yet, when it comes to distance learning, teachers often craft tasks that are entirely independent and individual. To make the most out of online learning, we need to leverage digital tools for collaboration.

Students can leverage the connective capacity of technology by collaborating with peers across the world through global collaboration projects. They can interview experts using email interviews or scheduled video conferences. In other words, they can break down the four walls of the classroom and engage with the larger world.

Access the Digital Download Shared Document Carousel Activity at newteachermindset.com.

Model the Process for Students

Ultimately, if we want students to use technology wisely, one of the best places to start is with our own practice. As teachers, you can share the ways you use technology as a professional tool. In the case of AI, you might use generative AI to design lesson materials and assessments. Let your students know how you start with the AI-generated option and modify it based on your knowledge of the content and your knowledge of them. Show how you fact-checked AI-generated text or corrected the bias within it. You might use AI to design a class calendar or clarify an idea.

Let your students in on the process. AI chatbots have now made differentiating instruction more feasible than ever (an idea we explore in the next chapter). Share this with students so that as they get older they can craft supports and scaffolds of their own. Generative AI can help save time and take our lessons to the next level. When your students see you model these creative ways of using generative AI, they have a role model for how ethical use looks as they move into a world shaped by machine learning. They learn how to make sure curiosity and creativity drive their own personal learning rather than allow the technology to do the heavy lifting. Here, students not only learn how to use the technology, but also how to retain their humanity in a world saturated by the technology.

On Pivoting

When the printing press was invented in 1440 and the world moved from handwritten scrolls to printed books, educators had to pivot. When calculators started solving math problems by simply pressing buttons, educators had to pivot. When the internet was introduced, we had to pivot. I remember in high school having to use a manual to create in-text citations. Now you can highlight a link in Google Docs and AI will generate it for you in perfect MLA format. You know what that means? We probably don't need those manuals anymore.

We've pivoted.

There's always road bumps along the way with any new change, but educators are used to those. It's in the nature of the work. But what doesn't change in education is its primary mission, which is to help students find success. Success as writers, thinkers, problem-solvers, mathematicians, researchers, creators, explorers—as people.

So in the constantly changing technological work, keep your eyes on that prize, and use the tools and resources at your disposal to do so.

Differentiated Instruction for Every Student

One time, two students who had a penchant for getting off-task were sitting in an area of my (Trevor's) classroom where I could keep a close eye on them. Max and Danny were supposed to be researching when I noticed Danny leaning over and looking at Max's laptop. I shot my glare across the room that said, "C'mon guys, stop watching YouTube videos and get back to work." Danny understood my look and replied, "It's not like that Mr. Muir. I gotta keep Max from having to go to summer school."

Oh, they were actually working. My bad.

I thanked Danny for helping out, and asked what they were working on. Danny said, "Everything. Max already has to take summer school for last semester, and I don't want him to have to for this one too." Max was sitting with his arms crossed, not open to the idea of me or Danny helping him out.

I said, "Max, I know you know this stuff. If you even work a little bit harder, you can pass this class and not have to take summer school."

Max mumbled something in reply, but I did not hear him the first time.

I said, "Say that again Max."

This time, nice and loud, he said, "I *want* to take summer school!"

I laughed because I thought he was joking. But he continued to cross his arms and made it clear he was not kidding with me. I asked, "Why would you want to take summer school when you can just get the credit now?"

Max replied, "I always take summer school. If I don't, I will go crazy. My mom doesn't let me leave my house all summer. Not even to go outside. It's the only way I get out."

I'd never heard that response for not working before, so I took a seat next to him and we talked a little more. I learned that Max was dead serious. He had actually failed all of his classes and gone to summer school every year of his entire life. All because his mom does not let him leave his house in the summer.

"Well, do you think if I called your mom she might loosen up a little?" I asked, "Would she let you out in the summer if you were to go play basketball with me and Danny?"

Max shook his head, "No way. I'm not allowed to leave the house in the summer unless it's for summer school."

I was speechless. Who is this mother? What is her problem? Doesn't she realize the impact her overprotectiveness is having on her son, who desperately needs to work harder in school, but also socialize and play in the summer months?

So I gave her a call, thinking I could persuade her to change the summer rule. And after saying some positive things about Max, I brought up the issue and asked her if she'd be willing to loosen up the reins a bit for him as motivation to work harder in school. I thought it was a pretty reasonable request.

She replied, "Absolutely not."

I was frustrated because clearly this mother does not realize what she's doing. She hasn't read the research on the importance of play for students and why they need to be outside. Max's mom must not know how vital socialization is, and how the hours in the summer I spent on my bike during childhood were some of the most formative of my life.

As I began to respectfully protest and make a case for Max's summer freedom, she cut in and said, "I'm going to stop you right there, Mr. Muir. I'm not letting my boy end up on the streets like his brother. And no teacher is going to talk me into it."

I was speechless again. It all started making sense to me. Max's mom loves her child more than her reputation. She is faced with a reality that if she gave Max the summer freedom that I had growing up in the suburbs, with the freedom and protection to roam the streets and catch fireflies at night, her son could be scooped up by a gang or by people and things that are beyond her protection. There's no doubt she realizes her son does not enjoy his school vacations sitting in the living room, but she'd rather have him bored and at home than lost and on the street or even worse.

Different Students Require Different Approaches

In this moment, I was exposed to a new world and a very unfamiliar reality. Max was smart, compassionate, funny, dynamic, and capable of achieving great things in life, yet was not getting to experience the success he is capable of. His circumstances had always influenced his success in school, and as a result, I needed to adjust my approach to teaching him.

Clearly the traditional motivators with Max were not going to be effective. If I expected him to respond to my teaching in the same way as every other student, I would be severely disappointed. His circumstances, motivations, and abilities are different from other students. And every other student has different circumstances, motivations, and abilities themselves. Because of this reality in every classroom, despite the location or socioeconomic conditions, teaching requires personalization, differentiation.

Does this mean teachers need to tailor their instruction to every single student and differentiate according to every one of their stories?

Good luck with that.

When I (John) was a new teacher, I had a goal of differentiating instruction for every student. I would provide additional directions, project sheets, tutorials, and small-group instruction for any student who needed help. My main focus was on providing the necessary accommodations on Individualized Educational Programs (IEPs) and 504 plans. I kept a list of specific strategies I would use in every phase of a lesson to help ensure that all students had access to their necessary accommodations. I also included language supports for English Language Learners (ELL) students, including sentence stems, vocabulary, and visuals.

This process was sometimes overwhelming in classes with 8–10 students who needed specific accommodations. I often had a nagging sense that I was failing to help some of my students who were not exceptional learners nor ELL but who still needed support. At one point, I made a goal of providing specific scaffolds for every single student based on their mastery of certain standards. But this became even more overwhelming.

Eventually, I made a small but subtle shift in my mindset. I provided all of the scaffolds to students and taught them to self-select the supports that they needed. I still had to monitor the process, but this reduced my workload while empowering students to be advocates for their own learning. When I made this shift, I found that students were more aware of their mastery. They seemed to persevere and continue more easily, and they grew more confident as learners.

Taking a Universal Design Approach

Initially, I struggled with allowing students to self-select the supports and scaffolds that they needed. What if a student used a support they didn't need? What if there was a delay with a neurodiverse student who failed to find the support they needed?

All of this changed when I worked with this amazing special education teacher named Crystal. She transformed the way I thought about scaffolds. One of her chief goals was that there would be no visible distinction between learners with exceptionalities (special education students) and the rest of the classroom. Similarly, she wanted co-teaching to mean that we both did direct and small-group instruction.

As she put it, "Inclusion needs to mean full inclusion."

My initial response was skepticism. "What if a student uses a scaffold that they don't need? What if general education students use an accommodation that's meant for a special education student?"

She responded, "Special education is a service, not a student. We teach students. We provide services." She then asked me if I ever used a curb cut or a ramp on the sidewalk.

"Yeah, they come in handy when I push a stroller." (My kids were little at the time.)

"Have you ever watched TV with closed captions on?" she asked.

I nodded. "All the time."

"That's universal design in our built world. Universal Design for Learning is similar," she said.

A little background on Universal Design for Learning (UDL). In the early 1960s, visionary architect Selwyn Goldsmith designed the initial curb cut, or dropped curb, to encourage people with limited mobility to have access to city sidewalks. It was part of a larger movement (led by disability advocates) toward universal access in the built environment by changing policies, systems, and structures to promote full inclusion. In the last few decades, architects, product developers, and user experience (UX) designers have embraced this philosophy of universal design. Coined by architect Ronald Mace, universal design is built on the core belief that we should design environments to be useable by all people, "without the need for adaptation or specialized design."

When you design for everyone, everyone benefits from the design.

This inclusive approach allows everyone to benefit from such designs. Hence, caregivers pushing strollers benefit from curb cuts. Similarly, viewers use closed captioning on videos regardless of hearing. In other words, when you design for everyone, everyone benefits from the design.

UDL applies this same philosophy of universal design to every aspect of learning, from learning spaces to materials to instruction and assessment to classroom culture and behavior management. Built around cognitive neuroscience, UDL is an inclusive educational framework that seeks to remove barriers while also keeping the learning challenging for all students. A UDL approach includes a paradigm shift from a deficit mindset to neurodiversity, from singular accommodations to universally accessible scaffolds and supports, and from a teacher-centric view to a student-centered approach centered on student agency.

Note that this self-selection process isn't always automatic for students. You might need to work with certain students on accessing scaffolds and self-advocating. Often, this works well as a partnership between a general education teacher and special education teacher. Earlier I mentioned Crystal, who would meet with students to help them set goals, identify strategies, and design systems for finding the necessary scaffolds. As the year progressed, her students would take on more ownership of the process until the point that she merely observed and answered questions only when necessary. Her goal was for her students to become self-directed learners.

What Does This Look Like?

The best approach involves a partnership with all teachers, including all general education teachers along with ELL and special education teachers. As a team, teachers can identify practical scaffolds and develop a plan for teaching students to self-select the scaffolds they need. This process might involve taking a deeper dive into an IEP, 504 Plan, or ELL/ESOL (English Speakers of Other Languages) documentation. But the idea is to seek out the expertise and advice from ELL and special education experts who can help general education teachers determine which scaffolds they might need. In turn, general education teachers can often speak into certain content area expertise and share some of their strategies they have found helpful. Here are a few ideas for how you might provide scaffolds that students can self-select. This is by no means an exhaustive list.

1. **Provide tutorials for all students.** This could involve a curation of tutorial videos in content areas or step-by-step directions with embedded .gifs that

explain the approach. While many of the tutorials will be academic, you might have tutorials for technology, for classroom processes, or for best practices in other areas (like best practices for video editing or podcast creation). The key idea is for all students to have access to these tutorials at all times.

2. **Incorporate anchor charts, visuals, and graphic organizers that all students can access at any time.** We can provide calendars and checklists as well as project blueprints that break down tasks for students. Similarly, you might want to provide slideshows ahead of time and allow all students access to the slide deck in advance. Each of these strategies can help students more easily break down information from working memory to long-term memory.

3. **Make small groups optional.** Instead of pulling small groups every time, create small tutorial seminars or workshops that any student can join. This helps prevent the stigma attached with small groups, while also sending the message to all students that it's okay to need a little extra help. In the process, students develop a growth mindset as they move through the challenges and shift toward mastery.

4. **Provide students with multiple methods for accessing the learning content.** This might include using multiple font sizes, closed captioning, text-to-speech technology, or the ability to change speed in audio and video. For example, you might pre-record direct instruction and play it for the whole class. However, students also have the option to slow down videos or audio (to .5x or .25x speed levels) to review the content again. While this flipped learning model can take more prep time, when you partner with other teachers, the process becomes more manageable.

5. **Provide flexibility with timing.** Too often, students internalize the notion that learning is all about speed and accuracy. When we are flexible with timing, students can work at different paces, making differentiation more of a reality. This might include flexibility on timing and due dates for assignments, but it might also mean additional think time or more opportunities for practice and retrieval during a lesson.

6. **Use front-loaded vocabulary ahead of time so that all students have access to the shared language of the content area.** You might do a total physical

response (TPR), use a Frayer Model, or use the Marzano approach. Whatever you choose, this front-loaded vocabulary allows all students the same access to the language. You can then use anchor charts, visuals, or an online shared document that students can access at all times when they are confused about a word or a concept.

7. **Provide sentence frames that any student can access.** Sentence frames can vary from hyper-structured to loosely structured. Typically, you have a portion that you provide and then a fill-in-the-blank area that students complete. For example, "One difference I notice about _____ is _____." You can provide sentence frames for entire paragraphs or for a single sentence. I've used them for peer discourse, for forming questions (especially in research), and as starters for writing assignments. While sentence frames (or sentence stems) are an ELL scaffold, I've found that any student struggling with complex or academic language can benefit from this scaffold. Similarly, you might provide sample sentences that they can modify on their own.

As educators, we want students to learn how to become self-directed lifelong learners. We won't always be available for students in every facet of life. So, when they learn how to self-select scaffolds, they learn how to find help on their own. They internalize the idea that getting help is a good thing and that they don't need to be helpless and wait for an adult to provide supports. In the process, they learn how to determine what they know, what they don't know, and where to find the strategies to access new learning. This allows them to plan their next strategies and monitor their learning. In the long run, they grow into the empowered, self-directed learners we know they can be.

Leverage AI for Designing Scaffolds and Supports

In Chapter 10, we mentioned that teachers can use generative AI as a professional tool. The following are a few ideas for how we can leverage AI tools to design scaffolds and supports.

1. **Leveled readers:** AI can generate reading materials at different levels of complexity, allowing teachers to provide students with texts that match their

current reading abilities. Here, a teacher might start with a nonfiction text at one lexile level, and then use generative AI to create multiple versions at other grade levels. Another option would be to provide an outline with general ideas and let the AI write the text. The teacher would then edit the text and use the AI to create multiple versions again.

2. **Checklists:** AI can generate personalized checklists based on a student's individual learning goals. These checklists can help students track their progress and stay organized. Similarly, the AI can break down a complex task or project into smaller checklists that function as a daily to do list. This can be a game-changer for students with lower executive functioning skills.

3. **Graphic organizers:** AI can create customized graphic organizers for different topics or subjects. These visuals aid in structuring information and making it easier to comprehend.

4. **Vocabulary explanations:** AI can generate explanations and examples for challenging vocabulary words, helping students better understand and use new terms in context. Visual generative AI can take these explanations and add pictures as well.

5. **Tutorials:** AI-powered tutorials can be created for specific topics or skills. Students can access these tutorials on demand to reinforce their learning. As a teacher, you might also keep a database of great online tutorials for students as well.

6. **Practice quizzes:** AI can generate practice quizzes and questions tailored to a student's current knowledge level. These quizzes can help students self-assess and identify areas that need improvement. If the quiz feels too daunting, you can create skill practice worksheets that students can opt into if they want more help. AI can generate math problems or science experiments tailored to a student's skill level, fostering gradual skill development.

7. **Interactive simulations:** AI can create interactive simulations or virtual labs that allow students to explore complex concepts in a hands-on manner.

8. **Adaptive feedback:** AI can provide real-time feedback on assignments and assessments, highlighting areas where students can improve and suggesting relevant resources. It can function like a personalized tutor, where students ask questions and get answers on demand.

9. **Peer collaboration matching:** AI can match students with peers who have complementary strengths and weaknesses, encouraging collaborative learning and support. Imagine the AI functioning as a silent partner helping a student during work. The key is to keep the help relevant and remain cognizant of learned helplessness. Earlier we mentioned productive struggle. Students still need this struggle even if they have AI to help them along.

10. **Personalized study plans:** Based on student performance data, AI can generate personalized study plans, recommending specific resources and activities to address individual learning gaps.

11. **Content summaries:** AI can automatically summarize lengthy texts or articles, making them more digestible for students who may struggle with reading comprehension. It can help to have students summarize the information first and then compare it to an AI-generated text summary and ask, "What did I get right or wrong?"

12. **Language translation and support:** For multilingual classrooms, AI can provide translation services and language support to ensure all students can access content in their preferred language.

13. **Text-to-speech and speech-to-text:** AI-powered tools can convert text to speech and vice versa, accommodating students with different learning preferences and abilities.

14. **Learning analytics:** AI can analyze student performance data and recommend appropriate scaffolds and supports as students progress through their learning journey.

Note that, in each case, you will begin with the AI-generated supports and you can edit them based on your knowledge. After all, you know your students and your context better than a machine. You know what they find engaging and interesting. You know where a scaffold might be confusing and need to be reworked. Here, you can take the machine-generated content and humanize it with your own perspective and insights. You can then empower students to self-select materials and supports that cater to their unique needs, thus promoting a more personalized experience for your students.

Small-Group Instruction

Do either of these scenarios sound familiar to you?

Scenario 1: A teacher teaches a lesson, and Student A learns what they need from it and now understands the key points. However, Students B and C do not demonstrate mastery, so the next day, the teacher tries a second attempt, and Student A has to sit through that lesson again even though they demonstrated that they were ready to move on.

Scenario 2: A teacher teaches a lesson, but Student A, despite their best efforts, just doesn't get it yet. They need the information again, or more practice, or for their teacher to give them more personal attention. But Students B and C demonstrate mastery, leading the teacher to believe that their lesson was effective, and they move on, even though Student A is not ready.

Most of us have felt the frustration of sitting through a lesson we did not need, or needing more instruction but not receiving it. The first scenario often leads to bored and frustrated students, and the second scenario can often lead to disheartened, embarrassed, and frustrated students. This is why small-group instruction is so vital in every classroom. Small-group instruction, also known as workshopping, is a chance for teachers to provide additional support to students who are struggling, or offering enrichment activities for students who are already proficient.

Thoughtfully Determine Workshop Participants

Identifying the students who should attend the small-group instruction is crucial. You can make these selections based on assessment data, ongoing formative assessments, or even making them optional for students. You can announce "If you feel like you still need a little extra help with this concept, I will be holding a workshop in front of the whiteboard in five minutes." Or "If you see a pink star on the assignment I handed back to you, you need to attend my workshop in five minutes."

Articulate the Purpose of the Workshop   Begin by setting clear objectives and explaining the purpose of the session. We can't stress this enough: make it clear to students that attending a workshop is not a punishment. The point of the workshop is to ensure that no one is left feeling frustrated or gets left behind.

Maintain Student Engagement   Engagement is key to the success of small-group instruction. Use interactive and varied teaching methods, incorporate visual aids, design hands-on activities, and use discussions and technology to cater to different learning styles. Encourage students to participate, ask open-ended questions, and provide opportunities for collaboration within the small group.

What you'll soon find is that students generally enjoy small-group instruction more than large-group. They are more intimate, personal, and less intimidating for students.

Check for Comprehension   Regularly assess students' comprehension during your workshops. Use formative assessment techniques such as quizzes, discussions, think-pair-share activities, or exit tickets to gauge their understanding of the material. When you provide immediate feedback to students, this allows you to adjust and ensure that students grasp the concepts you're teaching.

Keep Workshops Quick and Brief   Your workshops do not need, nor does time usually allow them, to be long sessions. Set a clear agenda and time frame for workshops. Focus on the most critical learning objectives and prioritize the content accordingly. Be concise and precise in explanations, emphasizing the most essential points.

Let's Talk about Gardens

Imagine a vast garden of flowers. They each bloom at their own time and pace. Some burst forth quickly in a riot of colors and fragrances early in the season. They are the tulips or crocuses, and it can feel like they were just waiting for permission to bloom. Call them show-offs, advanced, or just eager flowers, but regardless of their labels, they quickly fully blossom.

Other flowers in the garden take their time, unfolding their petals gradually. They are no less beautiful than the tulips, but they require longer days and warmer soil before they open up.

The sun shines equally on all, but each bud has its unique internal clock, waiting for the right moment to unfurl.

Just as a gardener tends to the diverse needs of various flowers, nurturing them with tailored care and attention, educators, too, must embrace the individual growth rates of their students. Each student is akin to a distinct bloom, needing the appropriate amount of sunlight, water, and nurturing to reach their full potential. It's the art of teaching to recognize and honor these differences, understanding that in this diverse garden of learning, every bloom will eventually showcase its brilliance in its own time and manner.

Small-Group Instruction Checklist

Here is a checklist to ensure that small group remedial instruction is targeted, engaging, and responsive to the unique needs of each student.

- Identify Learning Objectives:
  - Clearly define the specific learning objectives for the small-group instruction session.
- Assessment of Individual Needs:
  - Review assessment data to identify areas of weakness for each student in the small group.
  - Tailor instruction to address the identified gaps in knowledge or skills.
- Group Composition:
  - Formulate small groups based on similar learning needs.
  - Consider the dynamics and interactions among group members.
- Materials and Resources:
  - Prepare appropriate instructional materials and resources.
    - Technology needs?
    - Classroom supplies?
    - Texts?
- Adaptations and Differentiation:
  - Consider modifications based on learning styles, preferences, and abilities.
  - Plan interactive and engaging activities to maintain student interest.

- Incorporate varied instructional strategies to cater to different learning preferences.
- Monitoring Progress:
  - Establish criteria for success, and monitor individual and group progress.
  - Use formative assessment techniques to gauge understanding during the session.
- Questioning Techniques:
  - Develop probing and open-ended questions to encourage critical thinking.
  - Adjust questions based on the pace and comprehension of the students.
- Feedback Mechanism:
  - Create a feedback loop for students to share their understanding and challenges.
  - Provide constructive feedback on performance and progress.
- Scaffolded Support:
  - Provide scaffolded support, gradually releasing responsibility as students demonstrate proficiency.
  - Offer additional assistance to those who require more guidance.

Assessment Is More Than Grades

It was my second year of teaching and I (John) had one class period where 30% of the students were failing. I printed out progress reports and sent letters home to their parents and guardians. I pulled students aside, one on one, to explain why they might fail the class if they didn't try harder. I offered a reasonable policy. Any late work could still earn up to 75% of the grade.

Finally, one student shook his head and said, "Look, I like your class. I like what we do. I just don't care about turning in work."

"I see you working on it," I explained. "Do you need more time?"

He shrugged his shoulders.

"I can work with you," I added.

"*Work*? That's the word. I don't want to do the work. You treat grades like they're payment for work. You treat it like I'm an employee and grades will make students work harder. But what are you going to do? Fire me? I promise I'll turn in enough of my work to get a *D*. Nothing higher. Nothing lower."

I left that conversation rattled. It was the most honest student conversation I had experienced about grading. Here was a student labeled as TAG (Talented and Gifted) who actively participated in class, but simply didn't care about the game of school. He would earn just enough points for a *D* in every single class.

Later that day, I met with a friend who suggested that maybe this student had a point.

"Is the goal to motivate students to work harder or to provide accurate feedback on their learning?"

I got defensive.

"It can be both," I told him. "And if we want students to have the soft skills they'll need for the future, we need to reward hard work and sticking to deadlines."

Over the next few weeks as we continued this discussion, he challenged my thinking on assessment. He didn't say, "You're wrong." Instead, he asked me to explain my thinking. Was it possible that students might work just as hard with a mastery-based assessment approach? If I wanted to model it after the "real world," what did assessment look like in sports, in art, in music, in creative industries, and in engineering?

My mindset toward assessment slowly evolved. I continued to require students to turn in all work, but I quit taking off points for late work and instead treated late work as a discipline issue rather than academic one. I shifted my focus toward feedback and worked to align the assessments to the objectives. I encouraged students to retake tests and revise their work for a higher grade.

Still, my approach remained teacher-centered. I would grade student work and use that to modify lessons and pull small groups. I provided targeted feedback to help students determine what they knew, what they didn't know, and what they needed to do next. Here, assessment shifted from a teacher task to a conversation between the teacher and the student. However, it remained one-sided.

I knew that self-assessment and peer assessment were valuable tools for providing accurate feedback. But what if students were wrong? What if they gave each other awful feedback? What if a student didn't take self-assessment seriously? What if it was just a waste of time?

I was afraid to let go of control.

But slowly, I started adding little self-assessments in the form of surveys and self-reflections. I continued to do the grading, but students started engaging in more of the assessment process. We began to implement short, peer-feedback protocols as well. To my surprise, students took the process seriously. They provided practical peer feedback and engaged in honest self-reflection. There were some growing pains, but the key word there is *growing*. I watched them grow into more self-directed learners.

Five Reasons Students Should Own the Assessment Process

The following are five key reasons students should engage in frequent self-assessment and peer assessment.

1. Self-Assessment and Peer Assessment Save Time

In my first two years in the classroom, I spent anywhere from 15 to 20 hours a week grading papers. Sometimes I used a rubric. Other times, I focused on qualitative feedback. Often, I used both approaches together. While this was exhausting, I often felt like I wasn't doing enough. Students didn't seem to use the feedback I gave them to improve their work. They didn't seem to understand whether they had mastered the standards or accomplished the objectives. I worked tirelessly, but my students didn't seem to use any of the feedback I had given them.

As I shifted toward student-centered assessments, I began implementing one to three self-assessments per week. Some of these were simply self-graded quizzes or short reflections. Others were surveys or rubrics. By the end of the quarter, I launched our first student portfolio project. In the next semester, I began implementing peer feedback protocols for each lesson. Some of these were short, 1- to 3-minute turn-and-talks. Others were longer, like the 20-minute feedback system or the Harkness Protocol.

I soon felt a difference in my professional schedule. I spent fewer hours per week grading student work, but I still had all the data I needed to modify instruction and plan lessons. When I sat down to grade papers, I could provide deeper, richer feedback. Meanwhile, I had more time to plan lessons, gather materials, and conference with students. Because I didn't have to carry the entire assessment load myself, I was able to offer more frequent, targeted feedback during lessons. Assessment became fun. I know that's an odd word for it, but once it no longer felt frantic, I could finally *enjoy* providing meaningful feedback.

This had an immediate benefit on my students. I was more energetic and less stressed. I could spend more time providing authentic feedback and less time grading. Something else began to occur as well. I noticed that my students started using the feedback to improve their work. Because it was fully formative, they were less focused on a grade, and instead, focused on their learning.

2. Feedback Is More Practical When Students Own the Process

As teachers, we have a finite amount of time and energy. No matter how hard we work, we cannot grade every paper or provide meaningful feedback on every assignment. And yet, we know that the best feedback is timely, practical, and relevant.

When students engage in peer assessment, the feedback is immediate. There's not a one-week delay between turning in an assignment and receiving feedback. Students can focus on key areas of growth where they want to examine their progress and come up with next steps. This makes the feedback feel more relevant and practical.

This doesn't mean teacher feedback is irrelevant or untimely. As an educator, you are both a content expert and pedagogical expert. Students need your feedback in order to improve their skills and build on their conceptual development. There's actually a danger in using only self-assessment because students might not know what they don't know or what steps they need to take to improve. Similarly, peer feedback can backfire if it's too vague, overly positive, or inaccurate. It can create unhealthy power dynamics. For this reason, we recommend that teachers incorporate peer feedback but not peer grading, and self-assessment but not self-grading.

3. Students Improve in Their Metacognition

When students have strong metacognition skills, they are able to anticipate change and navigate complexity. But that doesn't always happen. According to a Pascarella and Terenzini study, one of the most significant challenges college students face is managing their own learning.[1]

However, it goes beyond success in college and career. If we want students to become lifelong learners, they need to know how to own their learning, which means they need to know how to think about thinking. I love the way the authors of *How Learning Works* put it, "To become self-directed learners, students must learn to assess the demands of the task, evaluate their own knowledge and skills, plan their approach, monitor their progress, and adjust their strategies as needed."[2]

The authors explain metacognition as a cycle (see Figure 12.1).

It starts with the ability to assess the task at hand. Here, students have a clear picture of what they need to accomplish. This part sounds easy. However, this goes beyond simply reading instructions. It includes the ability to integrate prior knowledge with new knowledge and make connections between direct instruction and a new tasks. If a task feels too complicated, students can become overwhelmed and give up. Other times, they might oversimplify the task or get hung up on one specific detail.

In the second phase, students evaluate their own strengths and weaknesses. This can be tricky if students have an inaccurate view of their skills. Often, students who are highly skilled will suffer Imposter Syndrome, where they underestimate their skills because they are painfully aware of what they don't know. On the other hand, students with a lower skill level might experience the Dunning Kruger Effect, where they overestimate their skills. This is another reason why

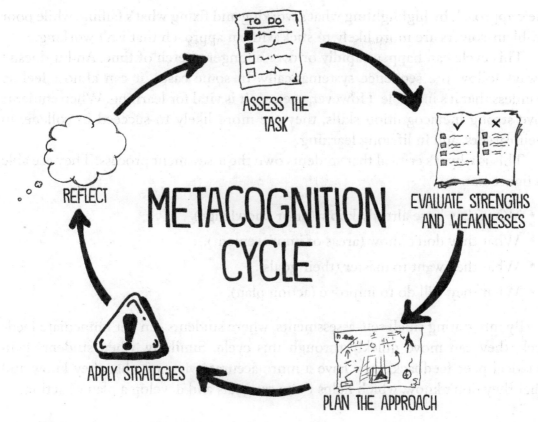

FIGURE 12.1 Metacognition cycle.

Source: Adapted from How Learning Works: Seven Research-Based Principles for Smart Teaching. Jossey-Bass.

peer feedback is so valuable. Sometimes a student needs to hear affirmation from a group of peers in order to develop a more accurate view of their strengths.

Afterward, students plan out their approach. Note that this does not have to be a detailed plan. In some cases, students might visualize where they need to be and what they need to do to get there. However, it's interesting that experts tend to spend more time in planning than novices, but are more effective in implementation because novices experience more initial mistakes.

Students then take action and apply the strategies and monitor their progress, which leads to the next phase, where they reflect on their learning and adjust their approach. Here, they might determine new strategies that ultimately lead back to a reassessment of the tasks. Effective problem-solvers are more likely to adjust their approach by highlighting what's working and fixing what's failing, while poor problem-solvers are more likely to stick with an approach that isn't working.

This cycle can happen rapidly or over a longer stretch of time. And it doesn't always follow the sequence systematically. In some cases, it can almost feel so seamless that it's invisible. However, even so, it is vital for learning. When students have strong metacognition skills, they are more likely to succeed in college, in their careers, and in lifelong learning.

This is why it's critical that students own the assessment process. They are able to figure out:

- What they have already know (prior knowledge).
- What they don't know (areas of improvement).
- What they want to master (their goals).
- What they will do to improve (action plan).

By integrating small self-assessments, where students can get immediate feedback, they can move quickly through this cycle. Similarly, when students gain practical peer feedback, they have a more accurate view of what they know and what they don't know, which helps them set goals and develop a plan of action.

4. Increased Buy-In Leads to Better Engagement

When students engage in collaborative work in my (Trevor's) class, I always have them fill out a peer and self-assessment to provide feedback on how everyone in their group collaborated during a unit or project. Students receive a simple rubric, score each other and themselves, and provide justification for their scores. My primary purpose for giving this assessment is to inform the collaboration score I'd input for each student at the end of a project. I always make it known to students that *they* are not determining each other's grades, but that I use these as tools to make my own determinations.

Then one time, at the end of a unit, a group presented its work to the class and I praised the entire group. As soon as I did this, a student in that group, named Emily, turned beet red and stormed to her desk and began to cry.

What did I say?

When I pulled that student aside and asked her what was wrong, she said to me, "You just clapped for my whole group, but I did all of the work!"

I responded, "I'm so sorry, I didn't know that. It looked like everyone was working the whole time." She proceeded to tell me how they were all faking it and taking advantage of her throughout the whole project.

After digging a little deeper, I realized I had been hoodwinked.

This was the moment where I learned that I cannot wait until the end of a collaborative project to find out if students were working effectively or not. From then on, I began to use the Teamwork Assessment, a tool for students to assess themselves and their teammates' contribution to collaborative work. Without notice, I'd give students the assessment to fill out. At first, many students were reluctant to give honest feedback as they were afraid of angering or alienating groupmates. However, they quickly learned the utility of this assessment. I wasn't just asking for their feedback to determine a grade anymore. Instead, I was asking for their input. Their ownership of this assessment now directly benefited them. Students like Emily no longer felt like they would be walked all over during a project.

When students own the assessment process, they have a greater sense of buy-in. There's a sense of control, or personal agency, in their learning. Students grow more aware of their progress as they navigate their learning. They're more aware of what they know and what they need to know. If you recall Chapter 8 on engagement, the key areas are commitment and attention. Self-assessment helps students stay committed through buy-in and learner agency. Meanwhile, they grow more aware of their progress, which can help improve their focus and attention.

Access the Digital Download Teamwork Assessment at newteachermindset.com.

Figure 12.2 is the simple Teamwork Assessment I give to students.

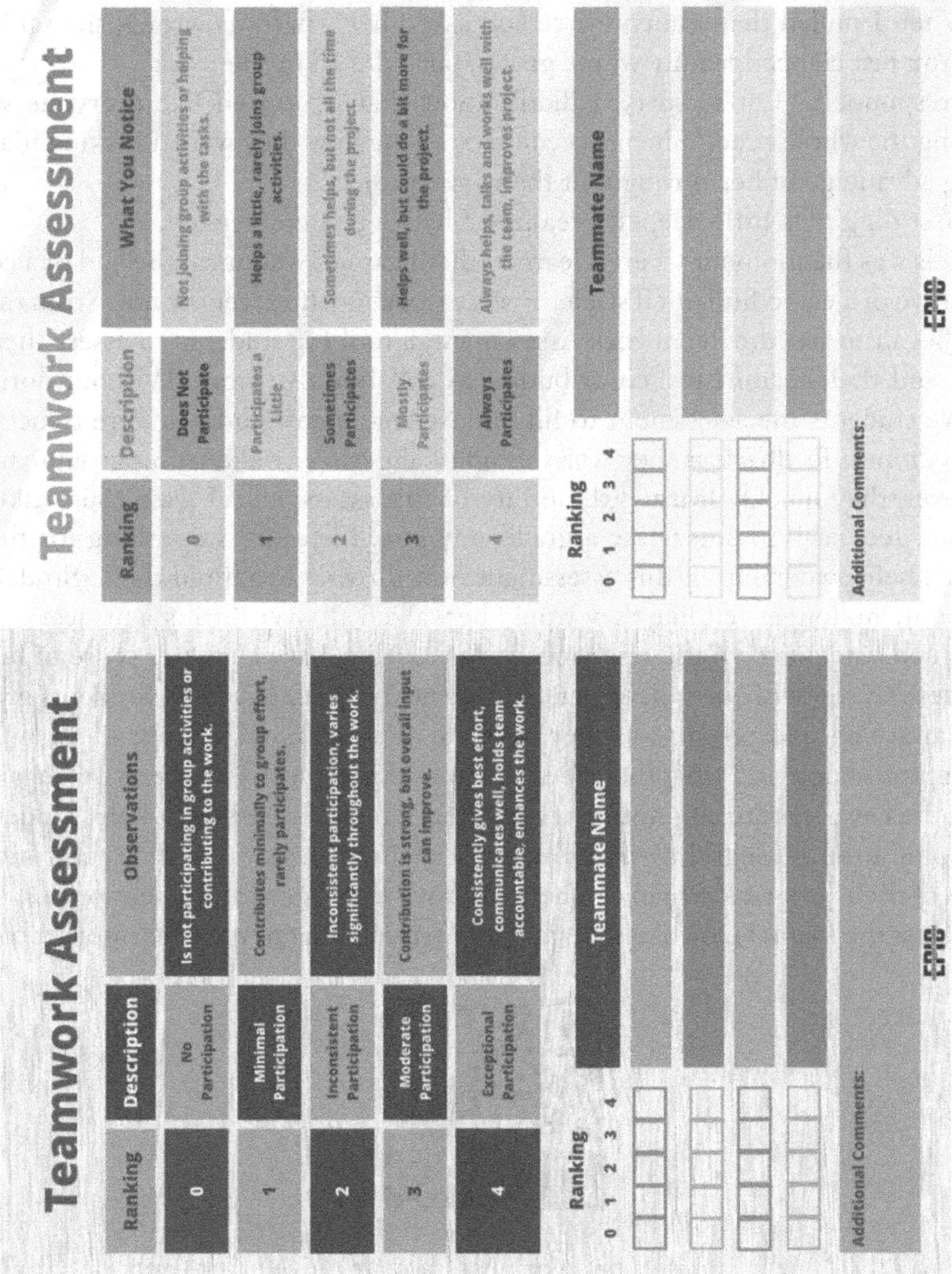

Teamwork Assessment

Ranking	Description	Observations
0	No Participation	Is not participating in group activities or contributing to the work.
1	Minimal Participation	Contributes minimally to group effort, rarely participates.
2	Inconsistent Participation	Inconsistent participation, varies significantly throughout the work.
3	Moderate Participation	Contribution is strong, but overall input can improve.
4	Exceptional Participation	Consistently gives best effort, communicates well, holds team accountable, enhances the work.

Teammate Name	Ranking 0 1 2 3 4

Additional Comments:

EPIC

Teamwork Assessment

Ranking	Description	What You Notice
0	Does Not Participate	Not joining group activities or helping with the tasks.
1	Participates a Little	Helps a little, rarely joins group activities.
2	Sometimes Participates	Sometimes helps, but not all the time during the project.
3	Mostly Participates	Helps well, but could do a bit more for the project.
4	Always Participates	Always helps, talks and works well with the team, improves project.

Teammate Name	Ranking 0 1 2 3 4

Additional Comments:

EPIC

FIGURE 12.2 Teamwork Assessment.

5. Students Develop Vital Lifelong Skills

When students own the assessment process, they grow in self-awareness and intellectual humility. They learn how to engage in goal-setting, how to monitor their progress, and if this is embedded within project-based learning, they learn project management. As students assess their strengths and weaknesses and try new approaches, they grow more resilient. They engage in iterative thinking and often come up with novel approaches for problem-solving. When students engage in peer assessment, they learn how to "be a good coach." They learn how to give and receive feedback. They learn how to collaborate and problem-solve. In other words, when we empower students to own the assessment process, we empower students to become lifelong learners.

Implementing Self-Assessment

When I (John) first began implementing project-based learning with students, I made the mistake of incorporating student reflection at the end of the project, but never really integrating it into the daily lessons. Students would do a long, multi-paragraph reflection as a way to process what they learned. Most students hated it for a few reasons. First, it was too long and skewed heavily into open-ended writing. Also, they couldn't really *do anything* with their reflections. After all, the project was finished.

I started thinking about my own projects. I'm reflecting all the time during the process. Sometimes these reflections are written. Sometimes I reflect by drawing ideas on a Sketchnote. Sometimes I journal. But other times, I merely think and reflect, and then move on. So, I changed my approach to include frequent, short, self-reflections with students. Here are some examples of the methods:

- **Silent reflections:** Sometimes all students need is a quick silent reflection. You can pause the class for two minutes and ask students to think about a particular prompt.

- **Open-ended writing:** Students can write their reflections in an open-ended way. Think of it as a stream of consciousness where the focus is on the thinking and not the quality of writing.

- **Lists:** While we tend to view written reflections as paragraphs, sometimes students might write their reflections as a list. An example would be something like, "Write out three things you have learned about yourself so far in this project" or "What are two takeaways from today and one question you have?"

- **Surveys:** Sometimes students struggle with open-ended prompts. With surveys, students can select from checkboxes (i.e., how are you feeling about this), give short numerical answers, or select categories that allow them to rate how they are doing. It's a more structured, quantified way of doing self-reflection.

- **Sketch your thinking:** This is a silent form of reflection, where students sketch out what they are thinking. One of my favorite options is a handout of a mind and the prompt, "Sketch what's going on in your mind right now as you think about this project."

- **Rubrics:** We tend to use rubrics at the end of a project, but they can serve as a great way to guide students in reflecting on their work as they compare their current work to the rubric criteria, and then diagnose potential issues and plan new strategies.

- **Checklists:** We don't tend to think of checklists as a form of reflection, but they allow you to reflect on how you're doing, which can then help you set new goals or determine next steps.

- **Progress bars:** Students fill out progress bars, where they shade a bar or a set of circles that represent their progress on a project. This might be their progress toward mastery in learning or it might be their progress toward completing tasks. We use progress bars all the time in life. If you've ever seen the movement circles on an Apple Watch or the progress bars in online forms, you'll notice just how prevalent they are in reflecting on your sense of progression.

- **Tracking goals:** Students create their own goals. Then they keep track of the progress. It might mean a graph, a progress bar, or simply a description of progress.

- **Concept map:** Students sketch out what they know about particular concepts.
- **The Assessment Grid** (see Digital Download).

Access the Digital Download Assessment Grid at newteachermindset.com.

By having students reflect more frequently with shorter reflections, they begin to internalize self-reflection as a natural, integrated part of doing creative work.

Implementing Peer Assessment

There's a reason so many students hate peer feedback. There's often a lack of clarity regarding what constitutes valuable feedback and how to provide it constructively and respectfully. Some students really struggle to offer any kind of critique for the fear of sounding mean. This uncertainty can lead to anxiety about saying the wrong thing or not being helpful. The fear of judgment plays a significant role as well. Students may worry that their peers will be overly critical or insensitive. This is especially true if a student feels insecure. Moreover, the peer feedback process can sometimes feel forced or insincere, as students may not genuinely understand each other's work or interests. Often, the peer feedback feels vague and overly positive, and there's no connection between the feedback and the actual revision process. So, here are some ways we can improve peer feedback.

Use structures to guide the peer feedback process.

On a more formal level, people sometimes use structures because the limitations of the protocol actually facilitate better feedback. Whether it's an art collective or a corporation, structured protocols can help facilitate better feedback. The following are specific structures you can use as students provide peer feedback:

- **The 20-minute feedback system:** This approach begins with one student sharing their work or pitching an idea while the other student actively listens. It has some elements that are similar to critical friends.

- **Structured feedback with sentence stems:** Here, you as a teacher provide specific sentence stems that your students can use to provide diagnostic, clarifying, or critical feedback.

- **5-2-1 structure:** This is simple. Students provide five strengths, two areas for improvement, and one question. If this seems like it skews heavily toward the positive, it's because we all have a negativity bias. In fact, researchers found it takes five pieces of positive affirmation to make up for one negative.[3]

- **Feedback carousel:** Each group gets a stack of sticky notes and offers anonymous feedback as they move from group to group.

- **Peer coaching:** Students interview each other about the process, using the coaching questions from the student-teacher conferences to guide them if they struggle to come up with reflection questions.

- **Mastermind:** This is a longer peer feedback structure. I'm actually a member of two different mastermind groups for blogging and one mastermind group for research and dissertation writing.

- **Rubric:** Students use the rubric (or a checklist based on the rubric) to give targeted feedback on how another student is doing.

Define the Criteria   Sometimes students struggle with peer feedback because they are unsure about the criteria for giving feedback. It can help to clarify the criteria for students. You might do this by showing a rubric and having students look at examples as a class. You might provide a checklist for students with the criteria set up in a list. You might have a visual that students look at as they compare peer work to the visual. It also helps to tie the peer feedback to the learning target or standard so that students can see how it connects to what they are learning.

Explain the Purpose of the Feedback   As we think of the larger scope of feedback, it's important for students to know what they are receiving feedback on and why it's important. Earlier in this chapter, we shared the metacognition cycle and how authentic feedback can help students learn to think about their thinking. As teachers, we sometimes need to make this explicit for students by sharing the following ahead of time:

- **What type of feedback you will give and receive.** Is it about the process or the product? Is it about the accuracy of knowledge? Is it about a particular skill?
- **The key areas where you want to focus.** In writing, it might be feedback on word choice. In a design thinking project, it might be feedback on the research students engage in. In math, it might be feedback on an approach to solving a problem.
- **What students will do with the feedback.** Remind students ahead of time what they will do when they receive feedback. In other words, how will students use the feedback they are giving and receiving?

You might provide students feedback on their ability to use the design thinking process in a project. Or you might provide feedback on their current product so that they can continue to revise and improve it. Students need to know both the parameters of feedback and the rationale. They should have a sense for why they are getting feedback, what type of feedback they are getting, and how they will actually use the feedback to further their learning.

Set Parameters and Expectations for Peer Feedback   While many students can be too nice in feedback, some students can be overly blunt or harsh. As teachers, we need to set the tone and parameters of peer feedback. It can help to set up norms in multiple areas.

- **Respectful language:** What are the types of phrases you want to use? What words or phrases do you want to avoid?
- **Active listening:** What does it mean to listen actively? What does it mean to listen with the goal of understanding? What does active listening "look" like? (*Note*: it's important we allow students to do this in a culturally responsive way that doesn't require eye contact.)

- **Focused participation:** What does focused participation look like? Have students visualize this by stating specific positive behaviors. Have them consider any distractions they might need to look out for ahead of time.

- **Preparation:** What does it mean to show up to peer feedback fully prepared? Is there work you need to bring? Are there questions you need to have?

- **Staying on topic:** What do you need to do in order to stay on topic? How do you keep focused on the feedback at hand?

After setting up the norms, you might need to have students review the norms before they meet for feedback. As students begin to internalize the feedback, you might not need to remind them of the norms every single time. In early elementary levels, you might need to model the use of the norms for students and even provide examples and non-examples. Younger students sometimes struggle to make the distinction between being mean and providing critical feedback. You might incorporate this idea into a social and emotional learning (SEL) lesson, and even cite examples you see from stories or picture books. This is a great conversation to have in a class meeting and then reference it during peer feedback.

Make Sure the Feedback Leads to Action

Whatever feedback protocol students use, they will ultimately need to summarize it and set up next steps. If they're providing feedback on a process, they might list changes they will take in future processes. If they're focused on a product, they can have a list of revisions they will make. If the peer feedback is more relational, they might have some ideas of how they will engage differently moving forward. But the key idea is that feedback has to be actionable for students.

An Empowered Approach

When we incorporate a student-centered approach to assessment, we increase student buy-in and ownership. As they engage in self-assessment, they improve in their metacognition as they ask, "What do I know? What is my mastery level? What do I need to do next?" As they engage in peer assessment, they determine key areas where they need to improve as they internalize the notion that feedback is a vital part of the process. This also frees you up, as a teacher, to save time and provide deeper, more qualitative feedback.

Notes

1. Pascarella, Ernest T., Terenzini, Patrick T. (2005). *How college affects students*, Vol. 2. Jossey-Bass.
2. Ambrose, Susan A., et.al. (2010). *How learning works: Seven research-based principles for smart teaching*. Jossey-Bass.
3. DealBook. (2013, June 14). Overcoming your negativity bias. *New York Times*.

You're Not a Superhero (And That's a Good Thing)

CHAPTER

You're Not a Superhero
(And That's a Good Thing)

In my (Trevor's) first year in the classroom, I had a student named Alonzo, who came from very difficult circumstances. Alonzo often came to school hungry and the staff took turns buying him breakfast every day. He'd have scars on his face from fighting, bags under his eyes from being kept up all night by fighting adults, and wore the same two outfits every single day. As a result of his own story, success in school was few and far between. His reading and writing skills were way below average, and he was extremely disruptive the first months of the school year.

As a fresh, young teacher, I made it my mission to help turn things around for Alonzo. I even declared to the school secretary that by the end of this school year, we were going "to save Alonzo." The secretary told me that's a great idea, but to remember that you can't "save all your students." She basically told me that there are some kids whom you just can't help, and so don't get down on yourself when that happens.

I nodded as if I agreed with her, but walked away from her desk sick to my stomach that anyone in education could have that perspective. If you don't believe that every kid's life can be turned around in school, maybe you should find another profession.

From then on, helping Alonzo became my top objective. I spent extra time with him during class, tutored after school, designed entire lessons around his interests. It was a slow train, but eventually it started moving. I started seeing progress in his reading and writing, but also watched him begin to enjoy his time at school. He began to feel safe around his teachers who actively cared for him, and I distinctly remember wanting to march up to the school secretary's desk and tell her I proved her wrong. You can, in fact, save all of your students.

But before I could do that, Alonzo's cousin was murdered, and Alonzo came to school the day after that happened absolutely distraught. The following day, Alonzo was absent. And then again the next day, and the rest of that week he did not show up to school.

The following Monday, Alonzo dropped out of high school. And the only other time I saw him again was about a year later standing on a street corner.

Many teachers start their careers with the goal of reaching every single one of their students. *If I just work hard enough, plan engaging enough lessons, and give every one of my students the attention they need, they will all be successful.* These are commendable intentions, and many people go into teaching because there was a teacher in their own childhood who pursued their success relentlessly, which led to real transformation. It only makes sense to want to do the same in others' lives.

However, while the notion of wanting to "save every kid" is common and noble, it's unattainable. Because the reality is that some students are not ready for transformation. There is often so much beneath the surface that finding success in your class is not yet possible. No amount of planning or effort can cause every student to engage in your class. As their teachers, this can be so disheartening.

Giving Yourself Grace

Alonzo's story made me wonder if I could possibly succeed as a teacher. It didn't seem to matter how hard I worked, how much time I spent, how much attention I gave, I could not save this kid. However, as demoralized as I felt after Alonzo dropped out, I continued to teach, and quickly learned that this story was not an anomaly. It turns out, for teachers, work often feels in vain. There are some students, because of a multitude of circumstances, who will not undergo any visible transformation in your class. For a while, this reality felt bleak. The school secretary was partially right; I cannot save them all.

However, I've learned since my first year that it's not my job to. What if the job of a teacher isn't to save anyone? Heck, what if your job isn't even to ensure your students' participation?

What if, instead, the work of a teacher is to continually give students the opportunity to succeed? Because the reality is: 100% participation is impossible. There are too many variables to achieve otherwise. You will encounter students at different stages of their stories, and sometimes, they are not ready for transformation. Realizing this is essential. Too many teachers feel inadequate because of the fact that the results of their work are not always visible.

My self-esteem took a huge hit the day Alonzo dropped out of school. But I've since realized that I don't know the rest of his story. I don't know if he re-enrolled in school, received his GED, or even went to college. I don't know if the attention I gave him made a permanent impact. I don't know if the reading and writing skills that he learned in my class stayed with him. Honestly, I have no idea where Alonzo is now or what he's doing, and I may never.

But I do know that he was given opportunities. His teachers were like gardeners. Some prepared the soil, others planted seeds, some watered, but none of us had the power to cause that seed to grow. That was out of our hands, and just because we did not see much more than a seedling break through the soil does not mean that it has not grown since.

This is a sometimes bitter reality of teaching. Teachers are not all-powerful, and no amount of innovative pedagogy or classroom technology will overcome that. And yet, this reality can also be liberating. Because ensuring 100% participation is impossible, you can give yourself grace when it does not happen.

I cannot save all of my students, but I can love them all. I can care for them all. I can design learning experiences with them in mind. I can give opportunities for them to succeed, and if I do that, I've done my job well.

The Superhero Mindset Leads to Burnout

When I started teaching, I wanted to be like a superhero. I wanted to be that teacher every kid remembers, the one students visit years after they graduate. I wanted to be the guy who gets invited to a hundred graduation parties and makes it to all of them. I wanted to be that teacher who actually got to know every one of his students, and listened to them when no one else will.

I wanted to be that person who could make grammar, or geometry, or photosynthesis, or the French Revolution come alive. I dress up like a Civil War soldier when teaching about the Civil War, and like Shakespeare during *Romeo and Juliet*. My classroom would be colorful and comfortable, and I'd burn candles so kids walking by in the hallway would smell French vanilla wafting from my room. I'd be a unique blend of Mr. Feeney, John Keating, Ms. Frizzle, and Albus Dumbledore. I wanted my evaluations to score as "Highly Effective" every year because I wanted to be the best teacher in the school.

When I got into teaching, I wanted to be the perfect teacher.

And then I actually started teaching and learned what the weight of this pressure feels like. But in my first couple years, I bore this weight almost like a martyr.

I ran myself ragged making sure every unit and every lesson was engaging and fun for my students.

I chaperoned every dance and never said no when asked to do something by administration or other teachers. I was calling home to parents every day, tutoring students before and after school. I was reading teacher books, doing nightly teacher Twitter Chats, listening to teacher podcasts on the way to work.

I refused to call in sick, and would hack my way through my lessons. I always smiled, and made sure kids knew that I loved my job and that I did it all for them.

And those difficult kids in my class, the ones who acted out but I could see behind their eyes that something was wrong, and that was why they were rude in my class? Well, I poured everything I had into them, and believed that if I worked hard enough, I could save them.

I was constantly striving for perfection.

And after several years of this, I burned out.

My tank was empty. I couldn't do it anymore. I was physically and mentally exhausted, and the result of this was me bringing a substandard version of myself to all aspects of life. I wasn't showing up with my best energy at school, but also not really having it at home either. I was like a candle burning from both ends, and that does not wind up well.

Five Ways to Tackle Perfectionism

Then one day, I grabbed lunch with my mentor. I remember sitting at Panera with bags under my eyes in front of this teacher of over 40 years. Somehow she still loved her work after more than four decades in the classroom, and I couldn't quite comprehend how. After patiently listening to me vent about all my perceived failures in the classroom, she said something to me I'll never forget.

She said, "Trevor, you don't have to be perfect."

I responded, "Yeah but—"

"No buts, you don't have to be perfect."

"But I want to change lives and for my class to be memorable—"

"Me too, Trevor, but you don't have to be perfect to do that."

I let her words sink in and sit with me, and that was when I decided to start over and make some important changes in how I approached teaching. I stopped relentlessly beating myself up when I lost my patience with students. There were times when I ran out of good ideas, and students had to learn about the French Revolution from reading a book, making the class a little boring at times. I stopped grading every single assignment. I still made time to listen to my students, but I started to create boundaries to protect my emotional health as well. And sometimes, I would turn off the lights during my planning period so I wouldn't have to talk to anyone at all.

I used up all of my personal days. I didn't always chaperone prom. I had to choose only three graduation parties to attend, disappointing the rest. As much as I knew how effective and important simulations, projects, or hands-on learning are, there were times when we did quiet, individual work in my class because I had papers to grade.

And you know what I discovered? You don't have to be perfect to get to know your students and build relationships with them. Perfection isn't required to make your class memorable and even fun. Heck, sometimes it won't be memorable and fun, and that's okay.

Students still learn and grow and fail and succeed in my imperfect classes.

I still strive to do my best and always get better at what I do. But I know I won't be perfect, and so don't have to carry the weight of trying to be. I don't know about you, but that's a heavy weight for me.

But with that weight gone, I find I'm a lot freer to be a better teacher.

The following are five strategies you can use to tackle perfectionism in your teaching craft.

1: Choose a Better Story

We both fell into a mindset that we had to save our students. But this mindset was actually fueled by a subtly dangerous story about what it means to be a successful teacher. We contrast the two stories as the *fireworks story* and the *campfire story*. Sounds odd, I know, but stick with us.

I (John) am lousy at trying to start a fire. Blame it on the fact that I never joined Boy Scouts or maybe the fact that "camping" when I was a kid involved hanging out in an RV. Whatever the reason, I always screw up a campfire. I begin too big, with large logs and lots of smoke. Sometimes I cheat by trying to douse the wood with lighter fluid. My wife, however, has it all figured out. It begins with smaller wood, some kindling and a little flame. There's always room to let the fire breathe. After a while, the fire grows until, without realizing it, we have something warm and powerful and capable of turning an ordinary marshmallow into something magical.

I'm not exactly sure how fire works, but it seems to be the opposite approach to fireworks. Fireworks are more entertaining—huge explosive displays of color, ear-splitting booms, the murmuring of "oohs" and "ahhs." Light a fuse and watch the explosion. It's instant and impressive.

I was thinking about this the other night while sitting in front of a fire pit. I was thinking about teacher movies. Each movie seemed to glorify the fireworks approach to teaching. The main character ascends to the furthest reaches of the sky and passionately explodes with huge results. All of a sudden students of poverty are doing calculus and falling in love with literature.

The Silverscreen Superteachers are impressive. They're loud and colorful and entertaining. Yet, like fireworks, the teachers featured in the movies only lasted a few years. I couldn't think of a single "based on a true story" movie where the true story didn't lead to the teacher leaving after less than a decade in the classroom. These movies were supposed to be inspirational, but the only thing they could inspire was a story of burnout.

I contrast this to my favorite former teacher, Mrs. Smoot. She was a teacher with a steady passion that lasted for decades. Instead of a loud, thundering message and a flashy display of lights, she provided warmth and created a space where a community could gather around. One is the fireworks story and the other is the campfire story. The following table contrasts the two different stories we tell ourselves as new teachers.

	Fireworks	Campfire
Protagonist	I want to be successful in quantitative, bold, measurable terms. I want to be known as successful.	I want to be faithful, wise, and humble. I want to be someone who loves people well.

	Fireworks	Campfire
Antagonist	Lazy teachers and lazy students	The lie of perfection
Plot	An amazing Hollywood-style story, something newsworthy and amazing	A small story filled with little daily things that make a difference over time
Conflict	Will I save the world? Will I make a difference?	Will I remain true to my convictions? Will I react in humility?
Theme	Make a difference	Be faithful and serve

I began my teaching career because I saw the job as meaningful. I wanted to do something that mattered. However, in my first year, after seeing movies like *Stand and Deliver*, I felt inspired to be a Superman swooping into the city and saving the day. I went from wanting to serve to wanting to make a difference. A big difference. The kind of difference that would make people marvel.

Armed with a handful of Hollywood prototypes, I now had a new story that involved both being perfect and expecting perfection from my students. I saw the antagonist as the other teachers who were pushing "low standards." My theme had moved from faithfulness to making a difference and being noticed.

Outwardly, this approach looked successful. Students were working hard and reading more challenging literature. We were filming a documentary. I had a philosophy club meeting each morning before school. However, I felt hollow. I became sarcastic toward students because I expected perfection. I grew overly critical of myself until eventually I grew critical of students. I felt like they owed me something. I snapped at students over the smallest mistakes. I was a disaster of a teacher.

A few weeks into this approach, I pulled my class aside and apologized. I did this for six class periods, and each time, I admitted that I had set unrealistic expectations for myself and for them. I had slipped into perfectionism and expected perfection from them. I had tried to be the superhero flying high above instead of staying grounded. To my surprise, the students responded with kindness and grace. It would take a little longer, though, for me to show myself the same kind of grace. In other words, I eventually chose the campfire story over the fireworks story.

2: Show Yourself Grace

When I was a first-year teacher, my mentor teacher observed me teaching a lesson. Afterward, we met up during my prep period and she said, "John, your lesson was outstanding but I want to talk to you about how you're treating someone in your class."

My stomach sank.

"What do you mean?"

"I've noticed that you are really good at showing students grace when they mess up. You encourage them to take creative risks. You remind them that learning is a process and mistakes are allowed. But then you turn around and demand perfection from someone else. You're really hard on him every time he makes a mistake. You're impatient with him and I can see that he's pulling back and isn't taking any risks. He's afraid."

"I haven't noticed. I mean, it's not on purpose."

"I know it's not intentional but it is damaging," she said.

"Who is it?" I asked.

"You," she answered.

I let out a sigh and cracked a smile.

"You seem relieved."

"I am," I answered. "I thought it was one of my students you were talking about."

"How is this any better?" she asked.

"I just . . . ."

"You have to show yourself the same amount of grace that you show your students. You expect them to make mistakes, but you get mad at yourself when you make mistakes. You're patient with them but you have no patience for your own learning curve. Take some bold risks. Fail hard and get back up and try again. It's the only way you're going to make it as a teacher," she said.

She was right. A simple strategy I started using was to ask myself, "What would I do if this were a trusted colleague? What would I do if this were a student?" It's been a long, slow journey, but I am learning to show myself the same type of compassion I would show a friend in a similar situation.

3: Learn to Say "No"

Saying "yes" is wonderful, and can lead to so many opportunities and adventures. But oversaying "yes" can drain us, overloading our limited capacity.

The problem is, if our own cups are not full, we will have nothing to overflow to our students. Teaching (and life) requires balance. Trying to be all things to all students is impossible. Instead, teachers have to set up structures and boundaries for themselves for the sake of their own well-being and that of their students.

After discovering being a superhero is unsustainable, as well as the wisdom imparted by mentors, I learned how to say things like:

"I'm sorry, I'm not able to stay late to tutor you today. But practice this at home and I can check in with you before school tomorrow."

And, "No, I don't have a big simulation or project planned this week; we are tackling the grammar unit."

And, "No, I can't coach the soccer team." "No, I can't chaperone the dance." "No, I can't be on that committee."

I learned to say "no" (which most superheroes don't do), and it did wonders for my emotional and physical health. The following questions might be helpful in evaluating whether to take on a new responsibility:

- Does this make me feel energized or does it drain my energy?
- Does this connect to my strengths and skills?
- Does this fit my personality and identity? For example, if you're an introvert, will this mean talking to too many people? If you're an extrovert, will you be alone too much of the time?
- Does this bring me joy?
- Does this fit my personal convictions and values? Does this fit with my deepest sense of purpose or is this merely something that looks good on a resume?
- Do I actually have time for this? Take the amount of time you assume it will take and double that. Do you still have time for it?

4: Set Reasonable Expectations for Yourself

In behavioral economics, there is a concept of the "planning fallacy." We tend to overestimate how much we can accomplish in a given time frame because we imagine our future actions in a perfect context free of mistakes. Letting go over perfectionism involves setting realistic goals for what you will accomplish. You don't have to grade everything. So, set a goal for how much you can realistically grade and then cut that number down by about a third.

Being a "Savior" Is an Unattainable Standard   Here's a hard truth: no matter how hard you work and how dedicated you are, you will never be perfect. This truth is hard because it seems so many people in society expect you to be perfect. Parents want you to be perfect for their kid. Principals want you to be perfect for their school. The school board wants you to be perfect for their district. Governors want you to be perfect for their state. But this standard is unachievable.

When we say things like, "My job is to change students' lives," or "I work with underprivileged kids," or "If not me, then who else will help them?," we are essentially putting our students in boxes they don't belong in. Whether a student comes from a rich or poor home, has involved parents or not, or lives in a high-crime neighborhood or not, they are more than these things. Every single student is a complex being with so much more than meets the eye.

The notion of "saving" students is especially dangerous in many low-income/Title I schools. When teachers adopt a savior complex, they often see themselves as the sole bearers of knowledge and solutions, positioning themselves as the rescuers of their students. This power dynamic can lead to an unhealthy teacher-student relationship where students are disempowered and discredited.

Even with what seems like the best of intentions, teachers can strip students of their agency and suppress their voices. Here, the teacher imposes their own values, norms, and solutions onto students, disregarding the diverse perspectives and lived experiences of those they are supposed to be helping. This often results in a deficit mindset about the students and their community and thus fails to acknowledge the autonomy and resilience of students.

By viewing them as beings who need to be saved, we are discounting their inherent value and contribution. We miss the dynamism they bring to school regardless if they have behavior or academic issues. We are boiling down the complexities of a student's life to categories that are far too small.

Rather than saving our students, I think we need to give them relentless love, and with that, opportunities. Opportunities for connection. Opportunities to be challenged and to grow. Chances to learn and succeed in a safe environment. By adopting this mindset, not only are teachers relieved of the duty to "save" their students, the students are not put into an unfair box with other students who "need to be saved."

5: Treat Your Lessons as Experiments

The campfire story is all about reframing success from perfect to faithfulness. I used to think that if I chased perfection, I would aim higher and reach a higher level of success. But over time, I realized that perfectionism actually leads to a lower quality of work. Here are a few of the results of perfectionism:

- **Unreasonable student expectations:** I start to believe that if I am working really hard to prove myself, my students need to respond in kind. I view it as a social contract where they owe me the same work that I put in.

- **No sense of humor:** I quit laughing. I quit smiling. I convince myself that there is no longer a place for joking in a profession where the stakes are so high.

- **Isolation:** I no longer work with others because I am trying to solve things on my own and prove to others that I am not weak. Moreover, without showing any signs of weakness, nobody knows that I am in such an ugly place, so they generally leave me alone. This fuels the sense of self-doubt about who I am as a teacher.

- **Misinterpretation:** A student misbehaves and I respond with the assumption that it's a personal attack on my character, when, in fact, that student is actually very social and simply wants to talk.

- **Lack of trust:** I quit trusting myself, my students, and my colleagues. I feel like I have to prove that I don't need any help. To be honest, there's no way they can trust me when I'm wearing the superhero mask because they don't even get a chance at seeing the real me.

- **Anger:** I get angry when others fail to perform up to my high standards and I get even angrier when I fail.

- **Risk aversion:** I become overly guarded in my approach, trying my best to avoid mistakes, because I haven't give myself permission to fail.

- **Resignation:** I give up. I teach without energy. I lose my passion.

That last one is what ultimately leads to burnout. After exploding in perfectionism, I am nothing more than a shell of a teacher, burnt out and falling from the sky. The good news is I can change course and opt for the campfire story. I can focus on being faithful. I can humble myself as a teacher. I can define *success* by standards that matter rather than focusing on test scores. I can remember that students don't need superheroes. They need compassionate adults who are dedicated to honing their craft as teachers.

One way to address this is by treating lessons as experiments. If success isn't based on the end results being perfect, I can take creative risks. I can try that epic project I dreamed up on the car ride home. If it fails, it doesn't mean I failed. It was merely a null hypothesis. I can take what I learned from the experience and apply it to my craft.

Being different means taking creative risks and reframing success to be about the journey and the mindset rather than the final student data. When things don't work perfectly, ask yourself, "Would I punish a student for this?" or would I say, "What can you do differently?" If you had a student who tried a new creative strategy that didn't work, would you affirm them for the effort they made or shame them because it failed to work?

Students Need Imperfection

In my first year of teaching, my friend Brad said something I'll never forget. I taught a lesson that tanked. It was awful. I literally did everything wrong. It was the cringiest of cringe and I shared every detail with him over a coffee.

I expected specific advice on how to fix the lesson. Instead, he said, "John, learning is like a seed. It's a mystery. And some teachers are like water. They nourish. They build relationships. They help students develop vital soft skills.

Others are like light. They impart wisdom. They stretch your thinking and push you intellectually. And then there's a third type. These teachers are manure. Total crap. I mean, the lessons stink. It's a total mess. Nothing works. With mentorship and guidance, hopefully they're not manure for long. But right now, total crap."

"Oh?" I asked.

"Yeah, but here's the thing. Kids need all of those. They need relationships and soft skills. They need critical thinking and academic achievement. But they also need to handle some crap to grow resilient."

I sat there silently thinking about my crappy lesson before he finally said, "And, John, here's the hard truth. You'll always be all three of those teachers, no matter how long you've taught. Light, water, crap. You're always going to be all of the above."

That's right. Sometimes we need the crap that becomes the fertilizer for growth. Our humanity is a gift to students.

The truth is, your students don't need a superhero. They need someone who can listen and learn and grow; someone who can admit their mistakes and move on. Which is way better than a superhero. You don't have to be perfect. Teaching is a craft that takes years to master, and even then, you'll continue to make mistakes.

And that's okay.

You are enough. You'll hear phrases saying teachers should do "whatever it takes," but actually you need boundaries and space and rest. You don't need to show up to every single sports event, sponsor every club, chaperone every single dance, join every committee, or grade every single paper students turn in. You don't need to be the first person to show up and the last person to leave the parking lot each day.

Teaching is exhausting. It's rewarding, yes. But it's physically and emotionally draining. Don't feel bad about leaving papers at your desk and going home and playing games with your kids or going for a run or having coffee with a friend or watching a movie or going hiking or reading a book that has nothing to do with teaching. Geek out on things that fascinate you. Pursue a creative hobby. Of course, you should care for every child and give them your energy and passion. But to do so, you need to refuel and find joy outside of the classroom. Doing so doesn't make you selfish. It makes you a better teacher.

There's a Difference between Superheroes and Heroes

Just because teachers should not try to be superheroes does not mean that they are not heroes. The expectation and pressure to be a savior for all students, demanding a teacher to sacrifice all of their time and energy for their jobs, is not realistic and it is not helpful.

However, when teachers find work/life balance, and therefore, have the capacity to teach their students well, heroic results often do happen. Adults 20 years later attribute their success to "that one teacher." Kids learn to read. First-generation students make it into college. Students become better people. Sometimes that student on the edge of dropping out does make it to graduation. The teacher who is dedicated to their craft and shows up every day to love, care for, and educate their students will have an impact.

Guaranteed.

But they also can leave at the end of the school day and not think about work when they get home. None of this is to say teachers can't be great, or that they shouldn't volunteer to chaperone dances or have epic lessons and projects for their students. Instead, it's to state that teachers do not always have to do these things in order to be the teacher their students need. So instead of wearing that T-shirt that says "I'm a teacher, what's your superpower?" just wear a dark one you don't mind spilling coffee on.

Self-Care: Teacher Care Is Student Care

One time at parent-teacher conferences, my student and his mother sat down in front of me (Trevor) at my table in the middle of the high school gym. I started our meeting by shaking the mother's hand and telling her how much I enjoyed having Thomas in my class. I said that Thomas works really hard, participates often, and is so kind to other students. However, the whole time that I was telling this mother about Thomas, I could see a grimace growing across her face. She just silently sat there in anger as I praised her son, Thomas.

So I paused and asked, "Is everything alright?"

The mother stared me down for another few seconds and finally said, "My son's name is Colin."

Oops.

I mixed Colin up with another student, and his mother was rightfully not too pleased about it. No amount of apologizing seemed to make her feel better either.

While I still get a pit in my stomach when I tell this story (I laugh about it, too, because that's just funny); I can pinpoint why it happened.

In the two months leading up to this parent-teacher conference, I had completed three massive projects with my students, sat on the school improvement team, chaperoned Homecoming, coached middle school soccer, ran a poetry club, taught five different preps, graded every assignment I assigned, and had a newborn baby at home.

My brain was fried. I was overextended, overcommitted, and absolutely exhausted. The result of this was mixing up students' names and making parents angry with me.

However, the larger result was my overall performance as a teacher. Because I was doing so many things and so little to care for myself, my energy was depleted in each of the areas I was giving it. My players on the soccer team were only getting a portion of my energy (and we lost all but one game that season). The teaching committees I was on received lackluster engagement. My students were experiencing a tired teacher. Even my new daughter was getting a substandard version of myself.

The adage "You cannot pour from an empty glass" was increasingly true in my life.

Teaching Is a Marathon

Between the demands at the beginning of the year to the urgency of spring testing season, the pace of teaching can sometimes feel like a sprint. However, it's much more like a marathon, involving extended periods of effort and challenge. And the result of this for most is being tired. At the end of this marathon each year, there are different levels of tired. Some people are simply exhausted. They have crossed the finish line and they are placing their hands over their head with a mix of gratitude that it's over and a sense of pride over facing a huge challenge. These teachers are worn out and need rest.

Other teachers are injured. These teachers have finished the marathon but they're hurting. Many are facing moral injury. What they have experienced is genuine injustice and it has shaken them to the core. Others have been traumatized. These teachers need more than just rest. They need healing. It might involve being part of a community dedicated to healing or it might involve sitting down with a counselor. It is imperative that educators take the time to identify whether they are tired or injured so they can take the necessary steps to thrive in their work. Figure 14.1 illustrates a continuum to help think through this.

In some cases, you need *rest*. Rest is a chance to recharge and take a break from your routine work. You might take a vacation, go on a few hikes, spend time with friends, read a book, spend a day baking, or binge-watch TV shows about baking. You might also engage in professional learning and work on some planning for the

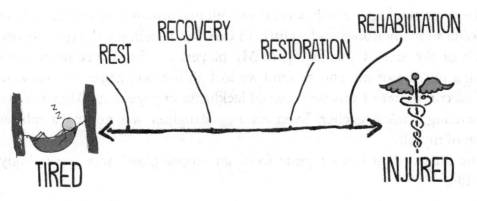

FIGURE 14.1 Tired-injured continuum.

next year, but it's still a break from the classroom. It boils down to engaging in the activities that reenergize you.

Next, there is *recovery*. Here, you might need a longer break with deeper processing. Recovery is more active than just resting. You might still have a vacation and spend time engaging in hobbies and being with loved ones, and even still engage in professional learning. But you might also need some time to reflect and journal or have coffee with a friend to process your work experience.

Beyond recovery, you might need *restoration*. Here, you recognize that something was taken from you this year and you need to recover it. In this phase, you still need to rest and recharge with time off. But you might also need affirmation. You might re-read old thank you notes from students or meet up with a colleague who will remind you that you are a great teacher even if this school year was a dumpster fire. This might even be a chance to celebrate the fact that you get to be in the same space as your students. It's a chance to look forward to the little things you've missed—like Socratic Seminars or hands-on maker projects.

Restoration is a chance to return to normal, but also a chance to redefine the new normal and advocate for changes in the system based on your found wisdom. But restoration might also involve seeking out professional help and therapy as you heal. It might involve leaving a toxic environment and finding a new place to teach.

It's important that we not only recognize where we are in this continuum, but that we also recognize where our colleagues are as well. We all need the permission to be in our own place in the journey of rest and recovery after a hard year.

Taking Days Off with Peace of Mind

So we've established that rest is a good thing, but sometimes taking days off can cause more headaches than they're worth. Because the reality is, if you are not with your students for a day, that means a substitute teacher is. And while substitutes can be brilliant, and are absolutely necessary educators, they most often do not have rapport with students. This, among other reasons, can lead to behavior issues. Part of actually resting on days off is providing yourself with the peace of mind that your class can still be productive without you present.

Leave Challenging Work

Often the reason for disruptions with a substitute stems from students not having anything to do. When making sub plans, it's easy to just divert to giving students simple activities or have them do review work. However, kids can smell busywork from a mile away. Instead, leave students activities that are just as challenging and enriching as if you were there. Tell students that if they have questions or problems to ask each other for help. And if they need you for an answer, to write it down and ask when you get back. This might be frustrating for students to have challenging work in your absence; however, they need to know how to work hard without their teacher present, and staying busy will also help keep them out of trouble.

Set Deadlines for the Work

Along with leaving challenging work, make sure that work has tight deadlines. Students should know that when there is a substitute, this does not mean there is time to be wasted in class. Have something for students to submit at the end of the class period or the first thing the next day. Also make sure the sub clearly announces the deadline for work so students know they need to maximize the time that they have.

Give the Class a Heads Up If Possible

No one can predict illness or absence for unexpected reasons. However, if you do know that you're going to be out the following day, give your class a heads-up. Let them know you are going to be out, and go over your expectations for them when there is a substitute. Talk about the work they will have to accomplish, let them know who the sub will be (if you know in advance), and remind them how they should behave even when you are not there. Hopefully, your words will still be in their heads the next day, and they'll be reminded of how much you value their positive behavior in your absence.

Compile a Strong List of Substitutes

In a perfect world, every substitute would be a former teacher who loves working with kids, knows how to manage a classroom, and loves to cover when teachers are out. However, I've had too many subs who simply read a book all of class or play on their phones. Sometimes these subs are fine because the class can manage itself and does not need any supervision. However, sometimes you need an adult in the room, a person who can help manage, be present, and engage with students.

This is why any time you come across a substitute with a strong reputation, you should get their phone number and email, and utilize them whenever you can. Build a relationship with them; send them a thank you email every time they cover your class. Understand how valuable they are to your students, and make them want to come back and keep serving your classroom. A list of strong substitutes is invaluable.

Missing school every now and then is inevitable. You will get sick, your kids will get sick, you'll attend a professional development, or you'll need a personal day. But being absent does not have to mean a day wasted in your classroom or that you will return to an angry note from a sub. It comes down to establishing a class culture that is strong whether you are there or not.

Find Community

One of the key indicators of a healthy person with a strong well-being is someone who is in community with others. Research shows that relationships reduce stress and even have an impact on physical health.[1] This is why it is so vital that educators stay connected with their colleagues. Few people beyond those who work in schools understand the daily pressures, stresses, and joys of being an educator. Teachers need people whom they can commiserate and celebrate with. They need elders for wisdom, younger ones for energy, people in the same boat as themselves to share and receive ideas.

As I was approaching teacher burnout, I realized how isolated I truly was. While teachers are surrounded by hundreds of students every day, it's easy to go a whole week without talking to another professional. When I started dedicating time to having lunch with others, stopping by the staff office, or even just sitting with someone else during my planning period, my mental health and well-being saw a huge improvement.

This isn't to say you need to become best friends with your colleagues (although teachers really do make great best friends), but being intentional with making these connections and maintaining them will bring more joy to your work and longevity to your career.

A Student-Centered Approach Helps Teachers

Throughout this book, we have shared practical ways to empower students to own their learning. When we do this, we help students develop the critical lifelong skills they need for the future. However, we also shift some of the load from the teachers to the students.

When we both shifted toward student empowerment, we noticed that we left school less tired each day. We no longer had to dictate every second of the school day because students needed less of us. Meanwhile, students were more tired. It was a good tired. It was active, engaged, excited tired. But it was still tired. As we shifted toward more of a facilitator role, we found that students were more active in every part of the learning process and we were able to focus on the key priorities that mattered most.

Here's what we mean:

- When students engage in self-assessment and peer assessment, teachers spend less time grading.

- When students manage their own projects, teachers can focus on whole class trends rather than have to micromanage every student.

- When students generate ideas, teachers don't have to bear the whole burden of coming up with highly engaging lessons.

- When students have ownership of the classroom routines and norms, teachers spend less time teaching procedures or correcting minor misbehaviors.

- When students engage in conflict resolution, it minimizes the emotional drain on the teacher.

- When students have classroom jobs, teachers spend less time on administrative tasks.

- When teachers design a student-centered organizational system, they save time and the class runs efficiently.

- When students self-select scaffolds, teachers reduce the stigma attached to being an exceptional learner while helping all students gain the support they need.

The journey of moving from teacher-centered to student-centered learning is challenging. It's hard to let go of some of the control we feel as teachers. But it went beyond the idea of control. This student-centered approach required additional planning at the beginning of the year. We had to design systems that would guide students in this process.

In other words, it was more work upfront but it became easier later. This investment was one made for student success, but equally one for self-care.

Breaking Up with Busy

When I (John) was a new teacher, I had a perfectionist mindset. I believed I had to give 110% in everything I did. I thought that the best teachers were the ones who arrived first and left last. I was a busy teacher, taking on all kinds of committee work and saying "yes" to every project. But then I had a moment when I decided to "break up with busy."

I arrived home from work and my five-year-old son was already holding a baseball.

"We can play, but I don't have a lot of *time*," I told him.

All I could think about was my to-do list. I had a department meeting to plan, papers to grade, and small projects to finish. However, as I slipped on the baseball glove, something changed. I forgot about my list and all I needed to do. Instead, we tossed the ball back and forth.

But even as we were playing together, my son kept asking, "Do you have more time?"

Do I have more time?

I couldn't answer it.

So, that night, I met with my wife and talked about my schedule. It was a hard conversation, where we talked about long-term priorities and what kind of a dad, husband, and teacher I wanted to be. I realized something critical: I was chasing perfectionism and trying to make a bunch of people happy and neglecting the people who mattered most.

That's when I broke up with busy. I quit some of the committees. I limited my projects. I set a curfew for myself at work. I learned when to give 110% and when to give 50%.

I was drowning in busy, and yet, I'd been wearing busy like a badge of honor, like I was winning some imaginary competition. But life isn't a game (unless we're talking about the board game).

But here's the thing: you don't get a trophy for packing your schedule with more projects and more accomplishments and more meetings. All you get is a bigger load of busy. But busy is hurried. Busy is overwhelmed. Busy is fast. Busy is careless. Busy is a hamster wheel that never ends and a sprint up the ladder without ever asking where it leads. There are moments when life gets busy. But I never want busy to be the new normal. I never want to look back at life and say, "Wow, I was really good at being busy."

I Became More Productive When I "Broke Up with Busy"

When I made the leap and decided to "break up with busy," I noticed something happening. I actually became a better teacher. After the difficult conversation with my wife, I remember thinking that I would be making sacrifices as an educator. However, that's not what happened. I actually had more time, more energy, and more mental bandwidth to be a better teacher for my students. It turns out that I was more productive when I was able to rest. Here's what I mean:

1. **I crafted better projects**. I finally had the time to prepare project-based learning unit plans and resources because I wasn't spending insane amounts of time inputting grades or putting together bulletin boards.

2. **I took creative risks**. Once I found the root cause of overworking, I began to experiment with student-centered learning and get over the fear of making mistakes as a teacher. I had already been shifting toward more authentic learning and design thinking, but now I felt the freedom to take it to the next level.

3. **I became more of a maker in my own life**. I began to engage in creative work in my spare time. For example, I started writing a novel, creating videos, and finding new hobbies.

4. **I shifted further toward student agency and empowerment**. I had already been asking the question, "What am I doing for my students that they could be doing for themselves?" I was on the journey toward empowering students with voice and choice. However, once I was truly able to "break up with busy," I took this student ownership to the next level by letting students self-select the scaffolding, engage in their own project management, and assess their own learning.

There's a difference between being busy and being productive. Being busy is about working harder, while being productive is about working smarter. Being busy is frantic, while being productive is focused. Being busy is fueled by perfectionism, while being productive is fueled by purpose. Being busy is about being good at everything, while being productive is about being great at a few important things.

The Power of Identifying Purpose

While narrowing down your task list and prioritizing your work can have a massive impact on your own well-being, there is still the reality that the regular tasks of being a teacher can have a draining effect. From student issues to negative parent behavior to administrative pressure, the work of educators is undeniably challenging at times. This is why understanding the primary reason for your efforts is so essential.

Researcher Dr. Angela Duckworth surveyed over 16,000 people who have achieved personal and career success in life with the goal of discovering a common denominator.[2] What do people with the tenacity and grit to overcome adversity and find success have that others do not?

Is it having a high IQ?

No correlation.

High pay?

No correlation (although probably nice).

Immensely talented?

No correlation.

A career with an easy job description?

No correlation.

What all 16,000 people had in common was a higher-level purpose. Dr. Duckworth found that people who know their efforts serve something bigger than themselves are far more motivated to overcome adversity to achieve success. Essentially, knowing and being able to articulate your work's purpose has tremendous power.

Of course, part of your purpose as an educator is getting paid and having stability. This shouldn't be minimized, and we need to continue to advocate for higher pay and better treatment of teachers. The altruistic side of a teacher's purpose should not nullify or invalidate in any way the practical needs of educators.

However, in order to truly thrive, teachers have to identify a purpose greater than just personal needs. According to Dr. Duckworth, the purpose must be "higher-level," serving something bigger than themselves. For teachers, the very name of the profession speaks of the high-level purpose of the work. Your work is to teach students content and skills to enrich their lives. It's work inherently based in service: you serve students, which serves their community, which serves society, which serves the world.

Understanding this, being able to articulate the elevated objective of your work, is one of the best ways to find success in it. It's one of the best ways to care for yourself. And the more detailed you can understand this purpose, the better.

Naming Your Purpose

Here's an exercise to name the higher-level purpose of your work as a teacher.

1. **Create a list of five ways you believe the world could be a better place.** This list will probably not take you long to come up with as there are countless ways the world can improve, so write your top five.

2. **Create a separate list of five tasks you regularly engage in as an educator.** Be practical with this list. You could include tasks like writing lesson plans,

leading discussions, small group instruction, arranging your classroom, and so on.

3. **Draw connections between your first and second lists.** Are there any ways you are helping make the world a better place (List 1) by performing the tasks on List 2? Even if it's incremental, is the world better because of your daily work?

 I'd bet it is. For instance, say you wrote on List 1 that the world would be better with no racism. Obviously you can't eliminate it yourself, but can you plan lessons that help students understand a better way of viewing and treating each other? Or if you wrote "less pollution" in List 1, are there ways to teach and demonstrate environmental responsibility in your class? Because if that's something you do, you are beginning a domino effect with your students. Through your daily work, you are helping address global issues in very real and practical ways.

4. **Once you've identified these correlations, take the time to write what stands out as most important to you.** Write what you believe is your deep, underlying purpose for being a teacher. You can use sentence stems like:

   - I help others. . . .
   - I create an environment where. . . .
   - I use my creativity and passion to. . . .
   - I help people discover. . . .

Rainy Day Folder

Now that you have your purpose identified, create reminders for yourself so you don't forget it. Write it on a sticky note, print it out and tape it to your desk, recite it before work each day. Keep it at the front of your mind. Purpose is a fuel for passion, especially when the passionate parts of teaching can be hard to identify.

 One thing to do on those particularly difficult days is to keep a "Rainy Day Folder." The Rainy Day Folder serves as a physical reminder of the purpose of your work. It is a folder to keep all of the notes and artifacts from past and current students, parents, other teachers, and administrators that affirm you as a teacher. Collect these notes and emails over time so you can return to them during hard times or at the end of a tough year.

Spending time reading through these treasures can remind you of your passion for teaching and why you got into it in the first place. These are why you decided to go through the education program and do all the work that it took to get into the classroom. If helping students discover success is your primary motivator, the Rainy Day Folder can remind you that success has happened.

Valleys and Mountaintops

Of course, we wish teaching was always gratifying, always full of brilliant moments. We wish our classrooms always looked like they could be featured on Pinterest, that our students would stand on their desks and recite poetry like they did in *Dead Poet's Society*, that we could leave each day tired but satisfied with the work we put in, but that's not what teaching really is. This work is often spent in the valleys. It can be messy, tiring, dull, painful, uninspired, and plain exhausting. It's in the valley that teachers begin to question if they are cut out for this line of work.

We think things like: "The teachers down the hallway don't have trouble getting students to turn in their work. But I do."

"I just can't keep up with all of this grading."

"I don't get paid enough to feel this kind of stress."

"I wonder what else I could do with my college degree."

And it's in the valley that around 16% of teachers are leaving the classroom every year. Call it teacher burnout, job dissatisfaction, overstress, or whatever you want; the fact is that this job can be difficult and too many talented professionals leave it. The reality is there's no way to eliminate the challenging aspect of being a teacher. The work is too messy, unpredictable, complex, and *human* to say otherwise.

However, another reality is that growth usually only happens in the imperfect moments. Think of it like valleys and mountaintops. While mountaintops are beautiful and the destination for most climbers, trees and flowers do not grow up there. There is nothing to sustain life. You can't stay at the summit forever; at some point, you have to make your way back down to the valley where the path is more treacherous, but also more abundant with life.

Surviving and thriving as a teacher strongly depends on the ability to learn and grow when times are difficult and having the patience waiting for the moments that make it all worth it. I (Trevor) remember a dreary February day when I had the unsavory task of giving my students an SAT practice test. I stood in silence for three hours as my students filled out bubble sheets while I looked out the window to see nothing but snow and gray skies.

I remember thinking that this is not what I signed up for. This isn't why I went to college to become a teacher. I became a teacher to inspire students and help them discover their dynamic and creative selves. I felt like a babysitter trapped by four walls, watching my students practice taking yet another test that only measures a small portion of their ability.

Sound familiar?

When the students finally finished the practice exam, I let them stand up and stretch a bit. However, one student named Jackson kept working at his desk. I said, "Jackson, you've been sitting for three hours. Why don't you get up and move around a bit?"

Jackson replied, "No, thanks, Mr. Muir. I'm almost finished writing this chapter of my book. I can't wait for you to read it!" And then he turned back to his notebook and kept writing.

Jackson was a student who, up to this point in the school year, had very little interest in school and zero enthusiasm for English class. That's why I was shocked—and overjoyed—to find him writing for pleasure after taking a three-hour exam. For me, it was a shot of adrenaline. It defined why I became a teacher. In the midst of this system that can, at times, hamper creativity and inspiration, Jackson was clearly inspired.

At some point in the school year, something I said or did helped give Jackson the push he needed to find this gift of his. All of a sudden, the snow outside looked beautiful. The gray sky made a soft background for the brick walls of our school building. The students in my class were laughing and talking with each other in a community formed by my classroom. I watched Jackson keep writing and felt like I made some type of impact on his life.

I was standing on a mountaintop.

Of course, I've stood on taller ones since: graduations, visits from past students, college acceptance letters, and so on, but this one was high enough to make me okay with going back into the valley. Moments like this are why you become a teacher—and if you can remember them, let them transform you, and shape your mindset—and are usually why you keep being one.

Discovering Mountaintops from the Valley

So here's the challenge: how can you find the joy that is often woven into the mundane? Discovering those little moments that demonstrate growth is, in fact, happening. Sometimes in education, we can get so consumed by final learning outcomes. The test scores, graduations, awards, and project showcases can be the dominant means of demonstrating concrete success. But here's the truth: a first grader finishing a page on their number role is a concrete success. Getting all 30 high school students to take out a book during silent reading is concrete. That kid who never says anything in class raising their hand for the first time is evidence of growth.

When we notice these moments, and truly reflect on the fact that students are growing, we can realize that the work in the valley is not in vain. We can know that despite the challenges, the work of a teacher is purposeful, powerful, and a career worthy of your time, talent, and passion.

Weekly Self-Care Checklist for Teachers

This weekly self-care checklist provides specific actions for each day, focusing on a balance between professional responsibilities and personal well-being. This is just a guide, so of course, adjust the activities based on your preferences and schedule.

- Sunday Evening:
  - Review Weekly Schedule:
    - Check lesson plans, meetings, and any important events scheduled for the week.

- Ensure all necessary materials, resources, and technology are prepared for Monday.
  - Organize Materials:
    - Arrange and organize teaching materials, handouts, and visual aids.
    - Confirm that all necessary resources are readily accessible.
  - Self-Care Planning:
    - Review self-care activities throughout the week.
    - Plan moments for relaxation, exercise, and personal enjoyment.
- Monday:
  - Take 10 minutes for a mindfulness/meditation/prayer exercise before the school day starts.
  - Read your personal purpose statement aloud.
- Tuesday:
  - Incorporate a brief stretching or yoga session to release tension.
  - Connect with a colleague for a short coffee break or casual conversation.
- Wednesday:
  - Delegate a non-essential task to a capable student or colleague.
  - Reflect on successes and challenges midweek, adjusting goals if needed.
- Thursday:
  - Engage in some sort of professional development.
    - Example: read a professional development book, join a webinar, attend a workshop, take an online course.
  - Set aside time for a hobby or activity you enjoy for at least 30 minutes.
- Friday:
  - Complete urgent tasks to start the weekend with a sense of accomplishment.
  - Celebrate achievements, big or small, from the week.
- Saturday:
  - Engage in physical activity, such as a brisk walk or workout.
  - Connect with friends or family for social support and relaxation.

- Throughout the Week:
  - Take short breaks during the day to stretch or practice deep breathing.
  - Maintain a healthy sleep schedule, ensuring you get adequate rest each night.
  - Avoid checking work emails or messages at nights and during the weekend.

Notes

1. Umberson, Debra, and Montez, Jennifer Karas. (2010). Social relationships and health: A flashpoint for health policy. *Journal of Health and Social Behavior*, 51(Suppl): S54–S66. doi:10.1177/0022146510383501. https://www.ncbi.nlm.nih.gov/pmc/articles/PMC3150158/
2. Duckworth, Angela. (2016). *Grit: The power of passion and perseverance*. Scribner.

The Public Side of Teaching

Most people have never ridden on a crab boat, and therefore wouldn't presume to tell employees on one how to operate it. They wouldn't give input on what tools and watercraft crabbers should use, how their boats should be arranged, and most would not scrutinize the profession as a whole based on the mistakes of a few crabbers. It's unfamiliar territory for most people, and so the formation of that occupation, what it looks like and how it operates, is left up to those within it. Most people who eat crab do not use their voices and resources to determine how it's harvested. The experiences, wisdom, and research from those within the profession do that.

Do you see where we're going with this?

Most adults have been through the education system in some way, shape, or form. Whether in a public or private school system, everyone has experience going to school. This fact, the reality that most of the 258 million adults in America alone have sat in classrooms and systematically learned from teachers, makes public input on the teaching profession very different than that of crab fishing.

From the media, to politicians, to social media, the general public often has a lot to say about how public schools operate. And this makes sense! The public has a vested interest in schools, including paying taxes to fund them. It is also one of the primary training grounds for the rest of life. The school experience has a dramatic impact on quality life. Research by the Virginia Commonwealth University shows strong correlations between education and having better health, more income/resources, and lower crime rates.[1] Schools matter, so community investments and input correspond.

The problem that arises is the fact that just because most people attended school does not mean they understand the inner workings of how they operate. The complexities of teaching are impossible to grasp without working in a classroom. As a result, social input is too often given from a place of ignorance. For example, the common quip about teachers getting the summer off is made by people who don't realize the professional development and planning teachers undergo in the summer, despite most teachers not receiving pay during those months.

It doesn't take long on social media to find people berating teachers or insisting that they operate in a certain way. If not kept in check, these external voices can have a dramatic negative impact on teachers and the schools they work in.

In a survey we conducted of over 2,600 teachers asking what the leading cause of teacher burnout is, the most common response was "feeling underappreciated and undervalued." Because everyone is invested in schools in some way, there is a public side to this profession unlike most others. The negative side of this reality is found in the damage to morale it can cause, as well as the uninformed policies and practices that result from non-educators regulating educators.

However, the positive side of this reality *is* that everyone has a vested interest in schools, and if critics can be transformed into supporters, that impact on teachers and their work can be enormous. Negativity toward education is often based on ignorance rather than malice, and so the more community members can learn about what actually happens in school, who is working in them, and what their motivations are, the veil can be lifted and detractors can become partners. When this happens, everyone can thrive. Let's talk about how to make this happen.

Value Every Voice in the Community

It was my (John's) sixth year of teaching, but everything felt new. I was in a new position (teaching photojournalism) at a new school. So, when I read the words "we need to talk" from my new principal, Raul, I panicked. I had just come from an environment where the principal had led from a place of fear and insecurity, and a "we need to talk" email often led to a loud berating and shaming.

I walked into the office and he waved me over to two chairs. Instead of starting with small talk, he went straight to the point. "John, I think the morning announcements have been working well, but there's one change I want you to make," he said.

I nodded.

"I notice that you don't have any ELL students doing the announcements. Why is that?" he asked.

"I, uh, well. It wasn't intentional. I put out a call for volunteers and those are the ones I chose," I pointed out.

He replied, "I know you value student voice, but that has to extend to *all* voices."

Honestly, I got defensive. I wasn't willing to listen to him. I started talking about language acquisition theory and affective filters and all of the research to back up my actions. I shared how my ELL students were afraid to go live in front of the school. Raul listened patiently to my response and then said, "If the system doesn't allow each student to have a voice, you need to change the system."

The conversation became even more challenging when we shifted to race and representation. Our school was about 90% Latino and close to 10% African American but there was no Black representation on the morning announcements.

"What message is that sending to students?" he asked.

We then talked about a plan of action. I modified the morning announcements by recruiting additional teams of students. I went directly to students with an invitation to join. I formed a student leadership team that would decide on the style, direction, and content of the announcements. Instead of going live, we prerecorded the whole show so that my ELL students could practice their lines ahead of time. We retooled everything so that students had more of a voice in the format and style of the morning show.

A week later, a teacher approached me in the staff lounge and said, "Can you do something about which students do the morning announcements? I can't even understand some of them."

At that moment, Raul walked into the staff lounge and said, "If you can't understand a student, maybe you need to work harder at listening."

Although I had never heard the term anti-racism, this was just a small example of what it was like to be in a school with leadership that valued our community.

Celebrating Diversity in Our Communities

Raul changed our approach to discipline. It started with the dress code, which he changed from uniforms to jeans and T-shirts. He refused to suspend students for wearing baggy pants or having skinny jeans (opposite ends of the acceptable denim spectrum). Later, when other schools were suspending students for dancing in the hallways (remember the Dougie?), Raul created huge dance competitions before school.

But it went beyond that. We also looked at the discipline data to examine bias and explore the racism within the system. I still remember when a teacher wanted to call the campus police (SRO) for a child being "disrespectful," Raul refused. There were still consequences, but they didn't need to be criminal.

Raul actively celebrated our community and challenged teacher perceptions about the neighborhoods around the school. When teachers said negative comments about parents in our community, he not only corrected them, but also made sure parents were part of the conversations on school improvement. One day, when a teacher went on a racist rant on social media, he addressed this teacher, but also asked teachers who were bystanders why they had been silent.

Raul built bridges between the school community and the local community. He often ate lunch with the custodial staff, the secretaries, and the aides. I can think of one member of the evening custodial staff who had dropped out of college to take care of his dying mother. Because Raul took the time to get to know him, the custodian went back to college to pursue his dream of becoming a teacher. Raul also started a leadership conference focused on building leadership capacity from within the community.

Raul invited White allies to listen more. To parents. To students. To experts who know and live this work. He challenged us to enter into hard conversations. It's easy to default to the ideas of "colorblindness" and to ignore or deflect. Raul's message was clear that we weren't just going to be tolerant or even pro-diversity as a staff. He was going to ask us to dismantle oppression in our daily practice as educators—something Trevor and I still often struggle with. We acknowledge that we are still on this journey.

When we think of community partnerships, we often think about parent volunteers or interviews with business leaders. But true partnership goes beyond merely connecting with the community and toward promoting equity and fighting oppression.

Viewing Parents and Community Members as a Resource

I (Trevor) once had a dream to build an aquaponics garden in a greenhouse attached to my classroom. Aquaponics is a form of gardening that combines raising fish in tanks with traditional gardening. In aquaponics, the nutrient-rich water (fish poop) from raising fish provides a natural fertilizer for the plants in the garden, which then help to purify the water for the fish. It's a really cool system that

I wanted my students to build, learning my class's content while raising fresh food for the local homeless shelter.

So I started planning and found almost everything I needed for my students to build the garden in my workshop at home or at Home Depot. The only thing I could not find was a 500-gallon container to raise the fish in. For several months I searched Craigslist, local stores, and even the junkyard to find a giant plastic fish tank. No matter where I looked, my search came up empty. The only tanks I could find were $1,000, and as a teacher, there was no way I could spend that kind of money, nor could I get my school to cough it up. When I announced to my class that unfortunately we would not be able to build the garden because I could not find a giant tank for the fish, one student raised her hand and said, "Oh, my dad has a bunch of giant clear tanks at our house that he uses for his business. I'm sure he would give us one."

"Wait, really? And you're telling me this NOW? I've been searching for one for months!"

Sure enough, after checking with her dad, he donated a 500-gallon tank to my classroom that we could raise fish in. This was after doing months of searching and almost giving up on the dream!

Caregivers Are an Invaluable Resource

This experience made apparent an invaluable resource I had at my disposal the entire time: my students' caregivers. If you have 25 students in any given year, that means you have at least 25 caregivers, with 25 careers, 25 interests, and 25 favors you can ask. And if you teach secondary, that number is often quadrupled or even more.

There is a common sentiment in teaching that this is an isolated career. Teachers may be surrounded by a bunch of students all day, but their connection with the outside world is limited and so they have to pull up their bootstraps and survive it on their own. What I began to learn when that student's dad gave me the water tank and countless situations since is the invaluable resource parents can be for the classroom. However, I also began to realize the benefit the community at large can have for learning.

Why Aren't Schools More Connected to Community Partners?

So if the community can benefit from students, and students benefit from the community, why does it often feel like there is a divide between them? Why aren't more schools intertwined with local organizations?

My guess is a lack of communication on the part of community members and the schools.

Teachers can and should boldly ask local organizations to be a part of what they're doing in the classroom. Whether it is sending a mass email to parents or even cold-calling or emailing an organization you found on Google, there does not need to be trepidation in making this connection. The truth is, I have never once as an educator been told, "No, I do not want to help your students" by anyone I've reached out to for help.

Not once!

Organizations have told me that now is not the best time and to check back in a couple months, but there has never been a refusal to connect with my students.

Community Members Benefit from Working with You

The reason I haven't been told "No!" is not just because I reached out to only altruistic, helpful people. While they have all been helpful and kind, it wasn't purely selfless. The reality is there are several benefits for organizations and businesses to connect with schools. I once did a project where my students partnered with a local college on a project. The dean of the school came and presented to my students and invited them to come share their work at the college. The college even paid for the buses for our field trip. It was an amazing experience for the students who benefited from an authentic audience at a real college.

And now several of the students in that class are currently enrolled at that college.

This project raised the engagement level for my students and raised the enrollment numbers for the college. It was a win-win. The same is true for any community partner you ask to work with your class. It's an opportunity for them to recruit future students, employees, and supporters. Partnering with schools is great PR for forward-facing organizations. It's also a chance for them to get fresh input from young people, which can assist their work.

This is why community partners want to be a part of the work your students are doing. They want to say "yes." But very rarely will the community get in touch with you to offer their assistance. Whether it is fair or not, it's the educator who often has to make that first connection. There is a classic adage used in the sales world that basically says, "You will never get what you want unless you first ask."

So who can you reach out to and ask to work with your students? What person or organization could help take your class to the next level and provide authenticity and expertise? And what community partners are out there that need you and your students?

You can use the simple email in the Digital Download to ask community members for their support of your class.

Access the Digital Download Reaching Out to a Professional at newteacher-mindset.com.

Curating Productive Voices on Social Media

Inviting the community to partner with schools illuminates what actually happens in classrooms, and can provide glimpses of what school can be when everyone invests their time and energy into them. However, 100% investment and understanding will never be a reality. In a time of divisive politics and loud social media, negative scrutiny will always have an aim toward educators. This is why educators have to develop practices to respond to criticism in healthy ways as well as shut out unhelpful voices in order to thrive in this profession for the long term.

Let's start with shutting out unhelpful voices. The internet can be an incredible resource for educators, but equally a negative space for them. Too often, its negative aspects overshadow the positive. The Pew Research Center found that the vast majority of people report that social media has a negative effect on them and the direction of society.[2] The reason for this can be found in the physiology of our brains. Neuroscientist Dr. Rick Hanson, says that our brains are like "Velcro for the bad and Teflon for the good."[3] Our brains are hardwired to absorb negativity far more than positivity.

This is why a wonderful day can be ruined by a single bad email at 5 p.m. It's also why it is so essential for educators (and everyone else) to regularly unplug from social media and avoid the negativity so present there. This might mean leaving platforms that have algorithms with inherent biases toward negativity. It also might mean curating whom you follow to only be people and pages with a positive bent toward education.

This doesn't mean only following voices similar to yours. We need exposure to differing opinions and ideas to continue to grow as educators, and social media can be a great place for that to happen. Instead, we have to ask if whom we follow can positively form our practices. Do they inspire you? Do they challenge you to think in new ways? Do they support schools, teachers, and students?

If the answer to these questions is "yes," then follow them on social media. If they only serve as a source of negativity, remove them from your social media life. Your brain is not meant to sift through that kind of negativity. It will hold onto it like Velcro, and that will impede your work with students. It may be time to stop following that guy from high school who loves to give his hot takes on the education system on Facebook. Maybe don't click on those news sites that only have headlines about the negative things happening in schools. Perhaps only follow Instagram pages that give you good ideas for your classroom, and unfollow the rest.

When you begin to curate uplifting, helpful media, your connection with the external school community will only grow, and your positive well-being will grow as well.

Parents/Caregivers Aren't the Enemy

Let's talk about parents.

I (Trevor) once had a student named Chris in my class who seemingly woke up every morning determined to terrorize me. Chris used to hide food in different places in my classroom so that they would rot and stink up the room weeks later. One time I found a cup of curdled chocolate milk behind *The Great Gatsby* on my bookshelf. He was constantly disruptive, and all of my proactive classroom management techniques had no effect on his behavior.

He was often rude, disrespectful, and worst of all, disruptive to the rest of the class. One day I finally had enough and sent Chris to the office and told him he was not welcome back in my classroom until he apologized to me and his classmates.

That afternoon during my prep period, I received a call from the front office that Chris's mother was on the phone and wanted to speak to me. I thought, "Excellent, she's probably going to offer to march Chris down to my classroom today after school and apologize. Just like my mother would have done with me."

So I answered the phone ready to offer grace and allow this mother to apologize.

Instead I heard this: "Mr. Muir, who do you think you are? Chris texted and told me how he is not welcome back in your class and how you hate him. And for what, a silly prank? I am meeting with your boss tomorrow and moving Chris to another class because this is unacceptable."

CLICK.

I was dumbfounded. How could this person just hang up on her son's teacher? Why didn't she at least ask me why her son was being disciplined? Does she really believe I hate her son and that I am banning him from my class? Seriously, she hung up on me?!

I was angry, and I felt like this encounter confirmed all of the stereotypes that modern parents carry. That they are petty, obstinate enablers who work against teachers as they try to mow down every obstacle that stands in the way of their children.

My anger was only amplified the next day when the parent demanded to my principal that I apologize to her for how I treated her son, and that I'd have to do it in person.

My blood was boiling that whole day as I awaited the meeting. Twenty minutes before Chris's mother arrived, my principal came into my classroom during my prep period and said two things to me, one that I loved hearing and one I couldn't comprehend.

First he said, "Trevor, this is bull crap. You disciplined Chris exactly how he should have been disciplined. It is ridiculous this parent thinks you should apologize to her."

And then he dropped the bomb: "Now you need to apologize to her."

Wait, what?! How could I seriously be expected to say sorry for doing the job she was supposed to do at home? I wanted to say that "I'm sorry for teaching your son some much-needed respect!"

The Secret to Working with Challenging Caregivers

My principal allowed me to air out my frustrations and then imparted wisdom that can only be gained after years of working with parents and students. He told me that this mom really loves her son. He said she cares more about him than anyone in the world, and would do anything to make sure he is safe and succeeds. He also said this mom doesn't realize that I have the same intentions for him, and that if I can make her realize this, if I can make her understand that I also want what's best for him, she will become an ally like no one else.

So I met with Chris's mom. And I started our meeting by swallowing my pride and apologizing for anything I may have done to mishandle the situation. Instead of making a bunch of excuses or listing all of the events leading up to Chris's detention, I said I was sorry for the way things transpired and that I was hoping she could help me find a way to get Chris back on track in my classroom.

Immediately, the tension drained from the room. My humility caught this mother completely off guard, and all of her anger and mistrust evaporated. She visibly relaxed her clenched muscles, and said, "Thank you so much for that. Chris really does love your class and I'm glad you are still open to working with him."

That was the moment that my principal's wisdom was confirmed. This mother didn't think I was a bad teacher; she was worried that I was a teacher who had given up on her son. As soon as she knew that I wasn't, we were able to have a great conversation. She opened up about the divorce she was in the middle of, and how Chris had been acting out lately because of it. She also apologized for his behavior and recognized how difficult that must've made my job. We came up with a plan for Chris, and she left on a positive note.

The Result of Having a Parent-Ally

The next day, Chris got to my classroom 30 minutes before school and apologized to me. He said sorry for how he acted all year and promised me he would do better. I was shocked by his own humility and thanked him for his apology. Later that day, I found out Chris was grounded for a month and his mother made him march in and apologize that morning. She had my back.

Of course, I think parents can be overbearing sometimes. John and I have both seen our fair share of difficult parents, and have even seen an uptick in this behavior in the past decade. This is why it's easy to slip into the mindset that parents are the enemy of teachers, that they will actively work against you, and that they hover over their children like helicopters.

However, dismissing them with a label misses out on a huge opportunity. The fact is, parents can be overbearing because they want what's best for their kids and do not always believe teachers share this same sentiment.

This isn't fair to teachers.

Teachers have enough on their plates that they shouldn't have to verbally express their devotion for their students and job to get respect and support.

But I do believe this is at the heart of overbearing behavior, and when we can make it clear to parents that we have their child's best interest at heart, and that this is the primary motivation for being a teacher in the first place, parents will begin to really do what's best for their kid, which is supporting their teacher. This is what happened with Chris.

Since my meeting with his mom, she became my No. 1 advocate. Not only did she support every further discipline I had with Chris (and there were more), but she was always the first to respond when I asked for parent volunteers. She went to bat for me with other parents, sent encouraging emails, and we never had a negative incident again.

Chris's mom became an ally. She was the opposite of an enemy. This is an attitude, a mindset we must develop toward parents. When they know you care about their kid, they will go to the ends of the earth to support you.

Here are a few ways to build rapport with parents and create strong allies for your classroom.

Communicate Often

During the school year, students spend more time during the week with their teachers than with their caregivers. Parents want to know what is happening during those eight-hour blocks when students are away from home. Communication is key. These are a few effective ways to communicate:

- **Create a weekly newsletter** to share what students are doing in your class each week.

- **Record short video updates** so parents can see and hear from their child's teacher regularly without having to come into school.

- **Share good news with caregivers.** Schedule two minutes once a day to call a parent and share a positive affirmation about their student. It can be as simple as praising a student for raising their hand for the first time. Take it from a couple parents: there's nothing better than hearing that someone else is proud of your child. Not only will this create strong allies, but this affirmation will make it back to the student.

- **Make phone calls.** For addressing student issues, sending emails is fine, but *phone calls are better*. Emails are easier to misinterpret and lack the ability for you to convey your tone and feelings as well as your voice. Yes, calling parents to have a difficult conversation may be intimidating, but you will get better at this skill every single time you practice it.

- **Encourage attendance at parent-teacher conferences.** Conferences are a powerful way to connect with your students' caregivers, but caregivers may not realize the impact they can have. Send an email a couple weeks in advance, sharing why these short meetings are important and invite them to attend.

Try This: Field Trip of the Community

Part One

It's important to know the entire community to make sense of the general attitudes of the city. Here are a few ideas:

- Take a bike ride through the neighborhoods. Soak in the smells and the scenes and the sounds.

- Go to the small grocery stores, the *carnicerias* and any other store that feels foreign to you.

- Consider attending a religious ceremony in the area. If you are teaching an ethnic group different from yours, you can appreciate the culture by seeing how they worship.

- Seriously think about living in the area. If you are a single first-year teacher, you might not have the constraints that others have in terms of mortgages and family obligations.

- Go to a community meeting—a Block Watch or a School Board meeting or any other place—where you can get to know the issues in the area.

Part Two

Reflection:

1. What are some of the values of the community? How are these similar and different to your own value system?

2. What type of culture shock did you experience? How might your students experience a similar or different culture shock when they go to school?

3. What are some of the hidden assets that the community has to offer?

Notes

1. Virginia Commonwealth University Center on Society and Health. (2015). Why education matters to health: Exploring the causes. https://societyhealth.vcu.edu/work/the-projects/why-education-matters-to-health-exploring-the-causes.html
2. Auxier, Brooke. (2020). 64% of Americans say social media have a mostly negative effect on the way things are going in the U.S. today. *Pew Research Center*. https://www.pewresearch.org/fact-tank/2020/10/15/64-of-americans-say-social-media-have-a-mostly-negative-effect-on-the-way-things-are-going-in-the-u-s-today/
3. The neuroscience of happiness. (n.d.). *Greater Good* magazine. Retrieved from https://greatergood.berkeley.edu/article/item/the_neuroscience_of_happiness

Conclusion

"It's just a dream," the teacher whispered to themself.

But it wasn't just a dream. It was a nightmare—the same recurring nightmare they had every August for well over a decade.

They found themself in a classroom, attempting to address the class, but it was like their voice was stuck on mute. Directions were impossible to give, their lips moved but their voice was trapped. The room loomed massive and bare. The classroom walls crumbled and cracked. Meanwhile, students were climbing on tables, shouting across the room. Some hurled items off the bookshelf. The principal walked in, holding a clipboard, shaking his head in disapproval of the teacher's perceived incompetence. He scrawled across his page, **Minimally Effective.** *Eventually, the teacher found their voice and yelled at the class, only to be met with laughter.*

This was their "first week of school" nightmare. A recurring dream every month before the start of a new school year where their subconscious revealed all the anxiety, pressure, and worries about once again stepping into the classroom. The dream had evolved over time with changing locations and characters, but the story remained the same.

What if the students refused to work? What if I have to raise my voice? What if the kids didn't take me seriously? What if I'm not prepared? What if angry parents call my principal?

What if I fail?

And these nightmares are not without reason. The truth is they'd become a reality throughout the teacher's career. Not all at once, but over the course of

243

nearly two decades, everything the teacher feared had happened. They had been unprepared and lessons had fallen apart. There had been moments when students mocked them; there was always "that one class" that seemed impossible to quiet down. They had yelled at a class in a moment of frustration. They had even been stuck on mute (it was on Zoom though, so an easy fix). And while classroom walls never physically crumbled, they felt the metaphorical squeeze due to the unjust lack of materials and equipment provided to a low-income school.

On a broader level, they had moments when they felt like they had no voice, choice, or control in their current classroom. No matter how much training they received, professional development books they read, or even how much experience they had in the classroom, being a teacher was still ripe with challenge.

And yet, none of these challenges broke them. It turns out there is a difference between failing and failure. Failure is the end. It's the breaking point where progress stops.

But failing is an opportunity. When you're a teacher, there's no possibility of getting it all right. Teachers are too human for that. There are too many variables, too many nuances, challenges, conflicts, and stories taking place. But amid all of this challenge is the opportunity to grow. And the longer you teach knowing this, the more you can observe the growth that takes place.

Yes, building relationships with students is messy. But years later when you hear from a former student who hails from a family with no one who has ever graduated high school tell you they earned a college diploma, you understand why the messiness is worth it.

When you make an adjustment to a lesson that failed miserably the first time, and see it move and engage your students, it makes the challenge of adapting worth the reward.

When you experience the joy of watching a child read for the first time, or see one speak bravely in front of their peers, or create something that causes real transformation in their community, or lean in to a difficult class discussion rather than shut down, or walk with a little more confidence thanks to an affirmation you gave, or you notice kids in your class are kind and inclusive, in part, because of the classroom climate you've created, you see why this work is worth it.

The impact teachers have on their students, both big and small, lasting and momentary, underscores the immeasurable value of dedicating one's life to education. It's in these simple joys and transformative moments that the true essence of teaching comes alive, reaffirming the profound difference educators can make in the lives of their students.

Therefore, we adapt. It's why we innovate. It's why we persist and develop resilience in a career that requires it in order to thrive.

The work of a teacher is important.

And perhaps this is why we have teacher dreams and nightmares. When an important task is looming, it tends to affect our conscious and subconscious. If you are approaching your first day ever as a teacher, you probably feel some anxiety. That makes sense because you are about to embark on critically important work.

And if you are about to start day one of your thirtieth year of teaching, you probably feel some anxiety. That makes sense because you are about to embark on critically important work. Of course you are nervous.

Day ones are a big deal.

But they're also not.

When we (Trevor and John) were new teachers, we both read books focused on the first few days of school. We learned about rules and procedures and desk configurations. The message seemed clear: make a great first impression. Set the tone for the year. If you fail in that first week, you'll be in recovery mode for the rest of the year.

Over time, though, we realized that the first week of school is overrated. It would be like only focusing on the wedding day and forgetting that life is found in all the days that follow.

The first week of school, as well as the first year of teaching, is the exposition in an epic journey.

It's the beginning.

Expositions matter, but epic journeys aren't found in the exposition. They occur after the inciting incident, as the conflicts intensifies and the characters develop and the plot thickens. It's okay to obsess over your "first day of school" outfit or rehearse your "first day of school" speech. But it's equally important, perhaps even more essential, to ask yourself how you'll continue to innovate and experiment and flourish on day 114, when you're exhausted and in need of inspiration.

In moments like those, and many more as a teacher, the work requires a different approach.

Being different isn't just about day one of your year or your career. It's about day 25 and day 4,025. It's the recognition that every day is an invitation to innovate. It's the freedom to make mistakes and learn along the way. It's knowing that you will always be a new teacher because you will always have a new group of students and a new context and new knowledge and new strategies in a constantly evolving world.

Being different is a mindset.

It's knowing that whether you are a pre-service teacher or one who has been in the classroom for decades, we all get to be new teachers. There is always the opportunity to approach this work with fresh eyes; to constantly explore, discover, fail, succeed, and grow for the sake of students and the world they impact.

Acknowledgments

hank you, Mrs. Reams, for teaching me to love writing. Thank you, Mrs. Choiniere, for giving me the confidence to read my writing aloud. Thanks, Mr. Bolander, for staying after school to help me with algebra, even though you weren't even my teacher. Thank you, Mr. Peters, for helping me get through my parents' divorce. Thank you, Mrs. Perry, for not allowing me to settle for anything less than perfection in my work. The MLA handbook still haunts my dreams, but I'm grateful. Thanks, Mr. Whitney, for demonstrating that teachers are storytellers. Thank you, Mrs. Bandy, for helping me believe in myself, and, Mr. Schuyler, for holding me accountable. And thank you, Mrs. Steelman, for showing me that even after 50 years in the classroom, you can still be a new teacher.

Thank you to every teacher who spent the time, energy, passion, expertise, and patience to help shape me into who I am today. You were and are a blessing.

—Trevor

My ideas, my stories, and my words are not solitary. There is a chorus of amazing teachers who shaped me in profound ways. Thank you to all of the teachers who believed in me, even when I didn't believe in myself. I want to acknowledge Mrs. Smoot, who inspired my love of history and who gave me the slack so I could develop grit. Eighth grade was the first time I ever experienced authentic project-based learning and I found my voice because of her. Thank you to Mr. Darrow, who taught me that research could be fun and that every act of creativity was an act of courage. Thank you to Mr. Allen, who helped me learn to see nuance in conflict. Thank you to Ms. Bedene and Ms. Waller, who inspired a love of nonfiction reading and who took the time to talk with me during my hardest, loneliest days of high school. Thank you to Mrs. Moore, who pushed me to become a better writer and a deeper thinker. Thank you to Mr. Weil, who knew that I didn't enjoy math and who patiently tutored me and worked with me and eventually helped me see that, actually, statistics is a pretty fun subject. Thank you to Brad, who mentored me as a new teacher and reminded me that success is about faithfulness and not test scores.

—John

About the Authors

Trevor Muir is the bestselling author of the books *The Epic Classroom* and *The Collaborative Classroom*. Starting his career as a high school teacher in a New Tech National Lab Site public school, Trevor was exposed early on to innovative and transformative teaching practices. At the heart of Trevor's work is sharing ideas and inspiration to keep moving the education system forward for the sake of students, their educators, and the communities they live in.

Drawing inspiration from his teaching experiences in middle and high school classrooms, as well as with pre-service teachers at Grand Valley State University, Trevor creates videos that have been viewed online over 35 million times. He also hosts *The Epic Classroom Podcast*, sharing weekly episodes covering a wide range of topics for educators. As the founder of EpicPBL, Trevor travels the globe helping teachers learn purposeful project-based learning. In his keynotes and workshops, Trevor uses the power of storytelling and research to inspire educators to thrive in their work.

For the past 10 years, Trevor has become keenly aware of the correlation between the investment in new teachers and their ongoing success in the classroom. This has led Trevor to conduct workshops, trainings, and create resources for emerging educators around the world.

Whether delivering the Promethean Keynote at the International Society for Technology in Education (ISTE) Conference; working with professors in Bogota, Colombia; or brainstorming with new elementary teachers in rural Indiana, Trevor is driven by the conviction that every student has the potential for greatness, and every teacher can be equipped to unlock that potential.

Trevor and his wife, Alli, live in Grand Rapids, Michigan, with their two children as well as a golden retriever named Zeke and a cat named Quimby.

Email: trevor@trevormuir.com

Website: trevormuir.com

Facebook: @epicclassroom

Twitter: @trevormuir

YouTube: @trevormuir

Instagram: @theepicclassroom

Dr. John Spencer is a former middle school teacher and current college professor with over two decades of experience in student-centered learning and design thinking. He explores research, interviews experts, deconstructs systems, and studies real-world examples of student empowerment in action. He shares these insights in books, blog posts, journal articles, free resources, animated videos, and podcasts.

As a full-time university professor, John works primarily with pre-service teachers in courses ranging from instructional design to classroom management to assessment and pedagogy. His goal is to empower teacher candidates to provide authentic and relevant learning experiences in a changing world. He also teaches courses on educational technology, pedagogy, and project-based learning.

John is the co-author of the bestselling books *Launch* and *Empower*, and the author of *Vintage Innovation* and *The AI Roadmap*. In 2013, he spoke at the White House, sharing a vision for how to empower students to be future-ready through creativity and design thinking. John has led workshops and delivered keynotes around the world with a focus on student creativity and self-direction. He frequently works with schools, districts, and organizations on how to design student-centered learning in blended, hybrid, and remote learning environments.

Email: john@spencerauthor.com

Website: spencerauthor.com

Twitter: @spencerideas

YouTube: spencervideos.com

Instagram: @spencereducation

Index

Page numbers followed by *f* refer to figures.